Basic Musicianship

LELAND D. BLAND
Wright State University

PRENTICE HALL, Englewood Cliffs, New Jersey   07632

Library of Congress Cataloging-in-Publication Data

Bland, Leland D.
  Basic musicianship / Leland D. Bland.
    p.   cm.
  Includes index.
  ISBN 13-066895-8
  1. Music—Theory, Elementary. I. Title.
MT7.B683 1988
781—dc19   88-23296
                                        CIP
                                        MN

Editorial/production supervision and
  interior design: Arthur Maisel
Cover design: Wanda Lubelska
Manufacturing buyer: Ray Keating

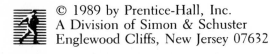 © 1989 by Prentice-Hall, Inc.
A Division of Simon & Schuster
Englewood Cliffs, New Jersey 07632

Printed in the United States of America

10 9 8 7 6 5 4 3 2 1

ISBN 0-13-066895-8

Prentice-Hall International (UK) Limited, *London*
Prentice-Hall of Australia Pty. Limited, *Sydney*
Prentice-Hall Canada Inc., *Toronto*
Prentice-Hall Hispanoamericana, S.A., *Mexico*
Prentice-Hall of India Private Limited, *New Delhi*
Prentice-Hall of Japan, Inc., *Tokyo*
Simon & Schuster Asia Pte. Ltd., *Singapore*
Editora Prentice-Hall do Brasil, Ltda., *Rio de Janeiro*

To Joyce and Doug

Contents

CHAPTER THREE

Introduction to Major Scales   38

CHAPTER FOUR

Fundamentals of Melody   58

CHAPTER FIVE

Melodic Variation and Improvisation Techniques   75
An Introduction to Composing Music

CHAPTER SIX

Intervals   85

CHAPTER SEVEN

Introduction to Minor Scales   102

CHAPTER EIGHT

Harmonizing Simple Melodies   125

Preface

Basic Musicianship represents a reevaluation of what is traditionally considered to be "fundamental" in music. In this new approach, "fundamentals" are defined as those structures which are most vital to the understanding of music. The text is based on the assumption that simple tonal music has order which can be easily understood by even the beginning musician. The unique order of presentation and a special format provide a smooth introduction to musical organization, with just enough detail initially to make the material understandable, but not overwhelming.

Several chapters are divided into two sections; the first section is an introduction to general ideas and musical procedures with appropriate practical applications, and the second is an expansion of those same ideas with attention to detail and more extensive drill. Such a format allows flexibility for (1) a general exploration of the fundamentals of tonal music, and, as desired, (2) a more in-depth coverage. For example, when major scales are presented in Chapter Three, only three common keys—C major, F major, and G major—are used in the first part of the chapter. The reader is then given the option of drilling on the remaining major scales, or turning to the first section of Chapter Four for an introduction to the "Fundamentals of Melody" in the three keys already learned. The latter option offers direct application of the concepts just studied. In Chapter Four, simple triad outlines in melodies, along with passing tones and neighbor tones, are introduced as basic melodic structures. Again, material for practice in additional keys is available.

The opening section of Chapter Five treats "Melodic Variation and Improvisation Techniques" in the three keys first learned in Chapters Three and Four. Consistent with the book's format, the second part of Chapter Five contains melodic study in additional keys. Exercises are provided for analyzing the performing musical examples, and even for creating variations from existing models. In Chapter Eight, "Harmonizing Simple Melodies," triadic melodies and elementary harmonization are interlinked.

Throughout the book, when technical details such as additional intervals, keys, and scales are covered, experience has already been provided in many important musical processes. Rigorous drill is encouraged only after adequate practice in applying concepts. In addition to the material composed especially for this partially programmed text, much of the music is taken from literature, including some songs from well-known musicals.

I would like to express my appreciation to the College of Liberal Arts at Wright State University for a grant to support the preparation of the manuscript. I also wish to thank Paul Magill for his care and skill in copying many of the musical examples and exercises.

Leland D. Bland

CHAPTER ONE
Meter
and Rhythm

Meter

Some of the most obvious ways to react to music are physical responses such as clapping the hands or dancing. Even subconsciously tapping the foot or nodding the head is a reaction to the *rhythm* or *meter* of the music. Listeners often describe their favorite music as having a "good beat," but although almost everyone refers to beat and rhythm in a general way, those who wish to understand the fundamentals of music need more precise meanings.

The concept of *beat* can be understood in relation to many simple activities. For example, walking at a steady pace with the same weight or emphasis on each step produces a series of identical sounds, or *beats*. If more weight is placed on one foot than on the other, a pattern alternating between loud and soft, or strong and weak, beats results. Such a recurring pattern of strong and weak beats is called a *meter in two* (Ex. 1–1a). A

EXAMPLE 1–1

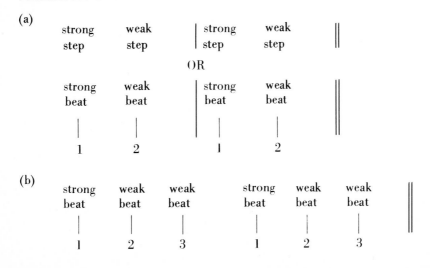

1

meter in three consists of a stress pattern of strong, weak, weak (Ex. 1–1*b*). (In many of the examples in this chapter, accents [>] are used to indicate strong beats. In musical compositions, however, these markings are usually placed only on notes that are to be given added stress.) The vertical lines in this example are called *bar lines*. These are used in musical notation to mark off the pattern of the meter, and the spaces between them are called *measures*.

Meter Signature

Music, like language, has written symbols to transmit the composer's ideas to the performer. One of the most common symbols for representing the beat is the *quarter note*, which consists of a notehead and a stem (Ex. 1–2). As will be seen later, the notehead also designates tones in a

EXAMPLE 1–2

melody. The *meter signature*, or *time signature* (Ex. 1–3), shows the number of beats per measure and the type of note that represents the beat.

EXAMPLE 1–3

Top number:	**3**	beats per measure
Bottom number:	**4**	note that equals the beat

A more graphic way to indicate the unit of the beat is:

The moderately slow beats in Examples 1–4, 1–5, and 1–6 are represented by quarter notes. The $\frac{3}{4}$ at the beginning of Example 1–4 indicates

EXAMPLE 1–4

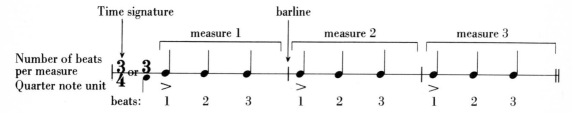

that there are three beats in each measure, and that the quarter note represents the beat. In Example 1–5, each measure consists of two beats, again with the quarter note as the unit of the beat.

EXAMPLE 1–5

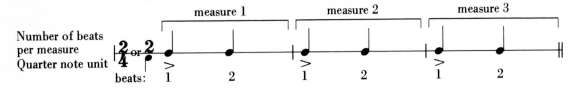

In Example 1–6, each measure contains four beats. Because the third beat is accented less than the first, the entire pattern in each measure is four beats long rather than two. Another way to designate $\frac{4}{4}$ meter is by using the symbol **C** (common time).

EXAMPLE 1–6

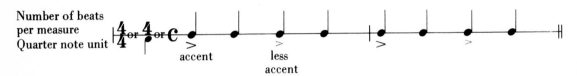

Conducting Patterns

The patterns used by conductors to convey beats (Ex. 1–7) are good visual representations that help performers feel the meter. While performing exercises and melodies throughout this book, you may wish to use conducting patterns to maintain a steady speed, or *tempo*.

EXAMPLE 1–7

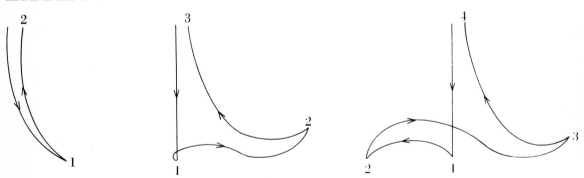

Tempo

The *tempo*, or speed, at which a composition is to be performed is given at the beginning, designated either with a term (often in Italian) or by a metronome setting. Some of the most common tempo markings and their meanings are as follows:

Largo   Very slow and broad

Adagio   Slow
Andante   Moderately slow
Moderato   Moderate
Allegro   Fast
Presto   Very fast

A metronome is a device which can be set to indicate the precise speed at which beats are to be played or sung. For example, the setting ♩ = 60 means that a quarter-note beat should occur 60 times per minute, or once per second.

❰ EXERCISE 1-1   Before clapping each of the following patterns, count a few preparatory measures to set the speed, or tempo. In the first one, for example, count aloud *one two one two* a few times at a steady tempo to establish the feel of the meter in two. Then perform the exercise, taking care to stress the appropriate beats. Follow the same procedure for clapping the other meters.

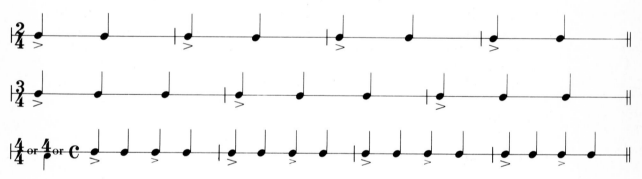

Place accents under the appropriate beats and draw barlines in the following:

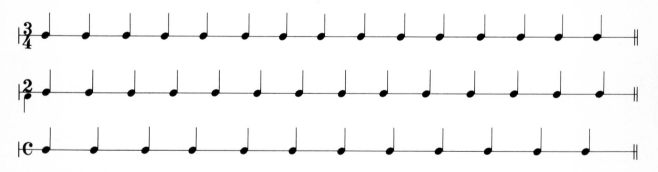

Rhythm

Rhythm is best understood in relation to setting words, or a text, to music. In Example 1–8*a*, the meter is $\frac{2}{4}$, the quarter note represents the beat, and the word "clap" is the text. To perform *a*, first count a measure or

EXAMPLE 1–8

(a)

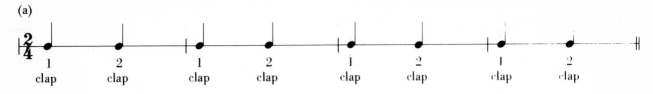

(b)

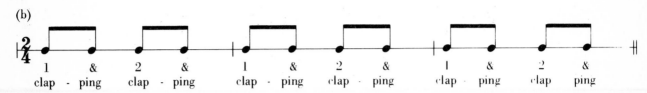

two aloud; then, without pausing, begin to clap the pattern. Next, clap it again but say the word "clap" on each beat.

Example 1–8*b* has the same meter as *a*, but the text has two syllables per beat. To accommodate the two syllables of the word "clap-ping," each beat is divided into two equal parts, or *duple division*. The quarter-note beat, then, is divided into two *eighth notes* (♫). Meters with beats that are divisible by 2 are called *simple* meters. After counting a few preparatory measures, perform Example 1–8*b* by clapping and saying the word "clap-ping." Sometimes musicians use a counting system such as "1 and 2 and" (1 & 2 &) to read simple subdivisions of the beat. As you do this, you may find it helpful to maintain the steady two beats per measure by tapping your foot.

◖EXERCISE 1-2

1. Before performing the following texts in succession, establish the $\frac{2}{4}$ meter by counting *one two* while tapping the foot in a steady pulse. Then, reading from left to right, clap the rhythms and say the words for each line without stopping. After you have had some practice, you may want to scramble the order of the lines.

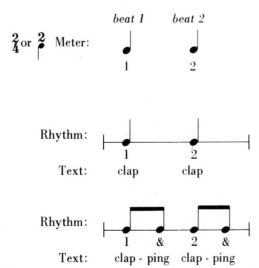

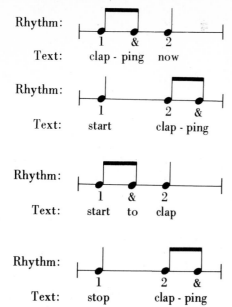

Rhythm:

Text: clap - ping   now
1   &   2

Rhythm:

Text: start   clap - ping
1   2   &

Rhythm:

Text: start   to   clap
1   &   2

Rhythm:

Text: stop   clap - ping
1   2   &

2. Set text phrases *a*, *b*, *c*, and *d* to $\frac{4}{4}$ meter. Start by tapping the meter while saying the text. Then, decide which words require quarter notes and which should have eighth notes. Check the result by performing your text setting.

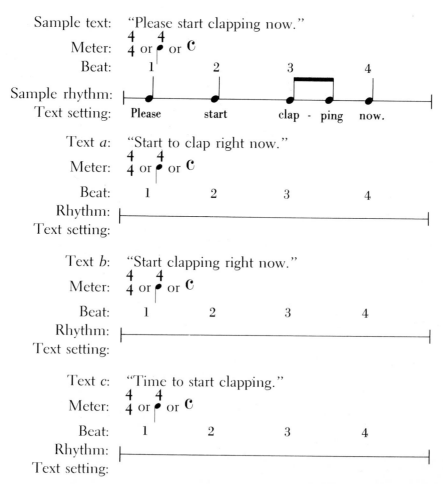

Sample text: "Please start clapping now."
Meter: $\frac{4}{4}$ or $\textbf{c}$ or $\textbf{C}$
Beat: 1   2   3   4

Sample rhythm:
Text setting: Please   start   clap - ping   now.

Text *a*:   "Start to clap right now."
Meter: $\frac{4}{4}$ or $\textbf{c}$ or $\textbf{C}$
Beat: 1   2   3   4
Rhythm:
Text setting:

Text *b*:   "Start clapping right now."
Meter: $\frac{4}{4}$ or $\textbf{c}$ or $\textbf{C}$
Beat: 1   2   3   4
Rhythm:
Text setting:

Text *c*:   "Time to start clapping."
Meter: $\frac{4}{4}$ or $\textbf{c}$ or $\textbf{C}$
Beat: 1   2   3   4
Rhythm:
Text setting:

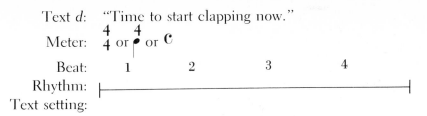

The natural flow of the text determines the meter and rhythm of the familiar Shaker song, "Simple Gifts." If you say the words in Example 1–9 a few times, you will notice a pattern of strong and weak accents. With the quarter note representing the beat, the pattern of accents fits $\frac{2}{4}$ meter.

EXAMPLE 1–9

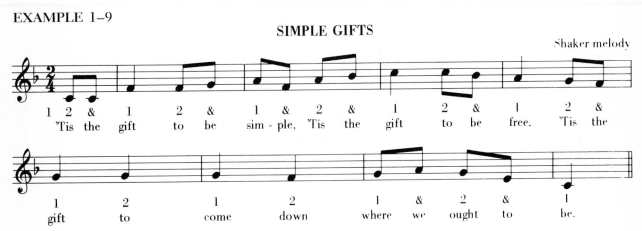

SIMPLE GIFTS

Shaker melody

Notating the rhythm of the words requires both quarter notes and eighth notes (simple division). The pattern of divided and undivided beats provides a good example for understanding the difference between rhythm and meter. *Meter* is the underlying series of strong and weak pulses; *rhythm* refers to the pattern(s) produced by durations of sound.

Notice that "Simple Gifts" begins with an incomplete measure, or *anacrusis*. Such incomplete measures are found in both vocal and instrumental music. Placement of the rhythm in the anacrusis is aided by counting a full measure rather than attempting to begin directly on the second beat with no preparation. Thus, following the indications under the music, count the first beat of the opening incomplete measure and then clap the rhythm of the words "'Tis the" on beat two.

Now perform the rhythm of "Simple Gifts," counting a few measures of $\frac{2}{4}$ meter in preparation.

Longer Note Values

The rhythm in Example 1–10 consists of quarter notes and notes of

EXAMPLE 1–10

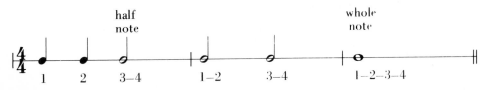

greater value. Two quarter notes equal a *half note* (♩♩ = ♩), while four quarter notes equal a *whole note* (♩♩♩♩ = 𝅝).

    The rhythm patterns of the text for "Hush Little Baby" (Ex. 1-11) in $\frac{4}{4}$ meter require quarter notes, eighth notes, and half notes. To perform this song, establish the feel of $\frac{4}{4}$ meter and then clap the rhythm.

EXAMPLE 1–11

To begin "We Wish You a Merry Christmas" in Example 1–12, count *one two* and say the word "We" or clap a quarter-note value on the third beat.

EXAMPLE 1–12

◖EXERCISE 1-3 Practice counting and clapping the following rhythms:

Quadruple Division of the Beat

In simple meters, subdivision of the beat into four parts is called *quadruple division*. The 1 & 2 & counting system discussed previously may be expanded to 1e&a 2e&a in order to create four syllables on each beat (Ex. 1-13). "Turkey in the Straw" in Example 1–14 contains typical subdivisions of the quarter note.

EXAMPLE 1–13

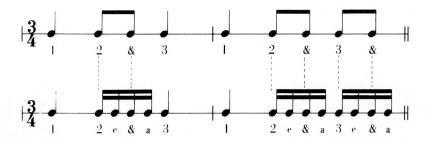

EXAMPLE 1–14

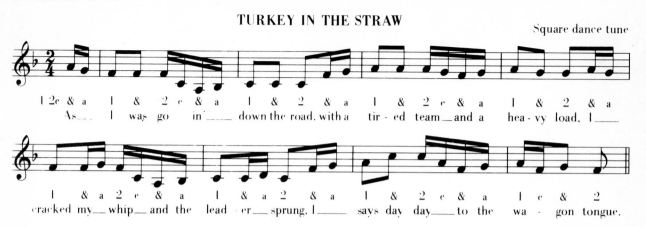

TURKEY IN THE STRAW

Square dance tune

EXERCISE 1-4   Practice counting and clapping the following rhythm patterns. Remember to establish the feel of the meter before performing the rhythm.

Other Rhythmic Values

Note values, both greater than and less than the quarter note, are summarized in Example 1–15.

EXAMPLE 1–15

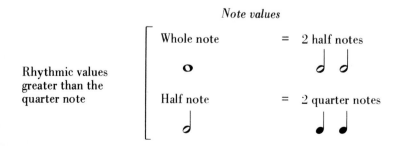

	Note values	
	Whole note	= 2 half notes
Rhythmic values greater than the quarter note	o	♩ ♩
	Half note	= 2 quarter notes
	♩	♩ ♩

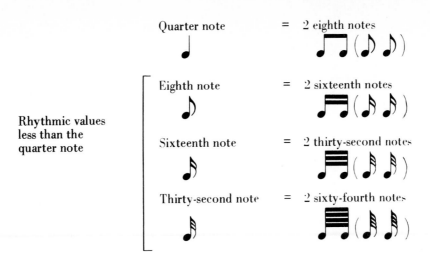

Rhythmic values less than the quarter note

Quarter note	=	2 eighth notes
Eighth note	=	2 sixteenth notes
Sixteenth note	=	2 thirty-second notes
Thirty-second note	=	2 sixty-fourth notes

Other Units for the Beat

Although the quarter note is the most common unit of the beat, other values are used frequently. Under certain conditions, music that looks on paper as though it should be in $\frac{4}{4}$ meter may be counted differently. For instance, the pattern in Example 1–16a has a meter signature of $\frac{4}{4}$. Because the tempo is *Moderato* (medium tempo), counting or conducting this fragment should cause no particular problem. In a faster tempo, however, counting or conducting the four beats per measure might be more challenging. This problem is easily solved by using the sign ¢, which stands for *alla breve*, or *cut time*. If the pattern in Example 1–16a is counted in *two*, as in Example 1–16b, a new meter in two is created in which the half note is the unit of the beat and the quarter note divides the beat. In fact, Example 1–16b would sound the same as a meter of $\frac{2}{2}$; compare Example 1–16b with c.

EXAMPLE 1–16

(a)

(b)

(c)

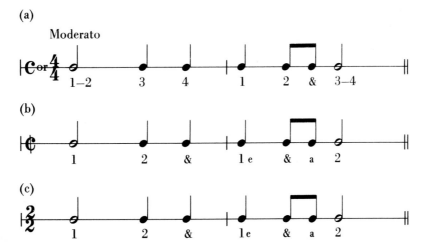

"The Drunken Sailor" in Example 1–17 is also counted in two, the half note being the unit of the beat, and the quarter note dividing the beat. As in the previous songs and exercises, set the tempo by counting a few preparatory measures and then clap the rhythm.

EXAMPLE 1–17

Other meters such as those shown in Example 1–18*a* through *c* are also used. In *a* the eighth note represents the beat; in *b* and *c* the half note and the sixteenth note represent the beat, respectively.

EXAMPLE 1–18

◖EXERCISE 1-5 Practice counting and clapping the following rhythms:

Rests

Although music is an art of organized sound, most compositions contain patterns in which "measured silence" is also an integral part. The symbol for measured silence is the *rest*; for every note value there is an equivalent rest duration. The quarter rests (𝄽) on the second and fourth beats in Example 1–19 have the same duration as quarter notes. In the $\frac{4}{4}$ meter in

EXAMPLE 1–19

EXAMPLE 1–20

Example 1–20, the half rest (▬) occupies two beats of silence, and the eighth rest receives one-half beat. For a list of equivalent note and rest values, refer to Example 1–21.

EXAMPLE 1–21

	Note value	Rest
Whole	𝅝	▬
Half	𝅗𝅥	▬
Quarter	♩	𝄽
Eighth	♪	𝄾
Sixteenth	𝅘𝅥𝅯	𝄿
Thirty-second	𝅘𝅥𝅰	𝅀
Sixth-fourth	𝅘𝅥𝅱	𝅁

Ties

The *tie*, a curved line extending between two noteheads of the same pitch,* connects two rhythmic values into one continuous sound. In Example 1–22a, the quarter note on the fourth beat of the first measure is tied to the quarter note on the first beat of the second measure, resulting in two beats of uninterrupted sound. Several practical reasons for using a tie are shown in Example 1–22a, b, and c.

EXAMPLE 1–22

a. Extending durations over a bar line

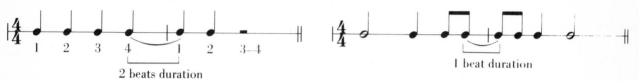

b. Connecting durations of unequal length

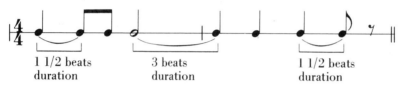

c. Clarifying placement of the beat

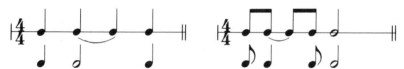

Dotted Notes

A dot after a note increases the duration of that note by one half its value. Some of the most common dotted notes and their equivalent values are shown in Example 1–23a, b, and c; typical counting patterns are given in Example 1–24a, b, and c.

EXAMPLE 1–23

(a) 𝅗𝅥. = 𝅘𝅥 + 𝅘𝅥 + 𝅘𝅥 or 𝅗𝅥 ⌣ 𝅘𝅥

(b) 𝅘𝅥. = 𝅘𝅥𝅮 + 𝅘𝅥𝅮 + 𝅘𝅥𝅮 or 𝅘𝅥 ⌣ 𝅘𝅥𝅮

(c) 𝅘𝅥𝅮. = 𝅘𝅥𝅯 + 𝅘𝅥𝅯 + 𝅘𝅥𝅯 or 𝅘𝅥𝅮 ⌣ 𝅘𝅥𝅯

*Pitch, which refers to the high or low quality of tones, will be discussed in Chapter 2.

EXAMPLE 1–24

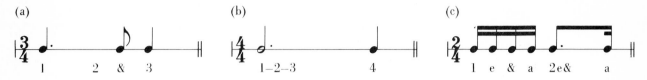

(a)　　　　　　　　　　(b)　　　　　　　　　　(c)

EXERCISE 1-6　Clap the rhythms of the following melodies. Reciting the words of these familiar songs will help you to develop a feeling for the placement of the dotted notes in the rhythm patterns.

AULD LANG SYNE

Robert Burns　　　　　　　　　　　　　　　　　　　　Scottish

count: 1 2 3 4　　1 & 2 & 3　4　　1 & 2 & 3　4　　1 & 2 & 3　4　　1–2–3　4
Should auld ac-quaint-ance be for-got, And nev-er brought to mind? Should

1 & 2　&　3　4　　1 & 2　&　3　4　　1 & 2　&　3　4　　1–2–3
auld ac-quaint-ance be for-got. And days of auld lang syne?

4　1 & 2 & 3　4　　1 & 2 & 3　4　　1 & 2 & 3　4　　1–2–3　4
For auld___ lang___ syne, my dear. For auld___ lang___ syne, We'll

1 & 2　&　3　4　　1 & 2　&　3　4　　1 & 2　&　3　4　　1–2–3
take a cup of kind-ness yet for auld___ lang___ syne.

AMERICA

Samuel F. Smith　　　　　　　　　　　　　　　　　Henry Carey

My coun-try 'tis of Thee, Sweet land of lib-er-ty,

of Thee I sing! Land where my fa-thers died land of the

Pil-grims' pride; From ev-'ry___ moun-tain side let___ free-dom ring!

Additional drill in dotted-note rhythms is provided below:

Clap the following song containing dotted eighth notes:

OH, SUSANNA

Stephen C. Foster

Additional drill in dotted-eighth-note rhythms is provided below:

The following rhythmic duets include rests, ties, and dotted notes. Have one individual or group perform the top line of each duet while a second individual or group performs the bottom line.

Compound Meters

Any note value may represent the beat, as long as the performer is aware of the composer's intentions. In "Greensleeves" (Ex. 1-25), the $\frac{6}{8}$ meter signature means that each measure contains six beats and that the eighth note represents the beat. The first and fourth beats are strong—the first slightly stronger than the fourth.

EXAMPLE 1–25

GREENSLEEVES

Slow   English

6   1–2 3 4–5 & 6   1–2 3 4–5 & 6   1–2 3 4–5 & 6   1–2 3 4–5 6
A - las,   my love__you   do   me wrong__ to   cast   me off__ dis - cour - teous - ly, When

1–2 3 4–5 & 6   1–2 3 4–5 & 6   1–2 & 3 4–5 & 6   1–2 3 4–5–6
I   have loved__you   you   so long__ de - light - ing in__your   com - pa - ny.

Depending upon the tempo, there are two options for counting or conducting music in $\frac{6}{8}$ meter. In a slow tempo, such as that in Example 1–25, each measure is usually counted in six beats. In a fast tempo, the individual eighth notes pass so quickly that the accented first and fourth beats tend to sound as two beats per measure. Each beat is then divided into *three* parts, or *compound division* (Ex. 1-26*a*). The unit of the beat, then, is the dotted quarter note (♩.). Counting in *two* is practical for the quick tempo of "When Johnny Comes Marching Home" (Ex. 1-26*b*).

Although both $\frac{3}{4}$ and $\frac{6}{8}$ meters may contain six eighth notes per measure, they differ in the placement of accents. While $\frac{6}{8}$ meter has two beats with triple division, $\frac{3}{4}$ meter has three beats with duple division. Compare the grouping of the eighth notes in Example 1–27*a* with that in *b*.

EXAMPLE 1–26

(a)

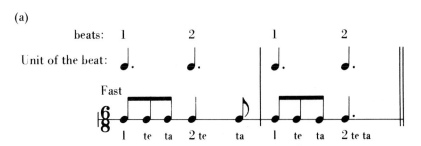

beats: 1   2   1   2

Unit of the beat: ♩.   ♩.   ♩.   ♩.

Fast

1 te ta   2 te   ta   1 te ta   2 te ta

(b)

WHEN JOHNNY COMES MARCHING HOME

American

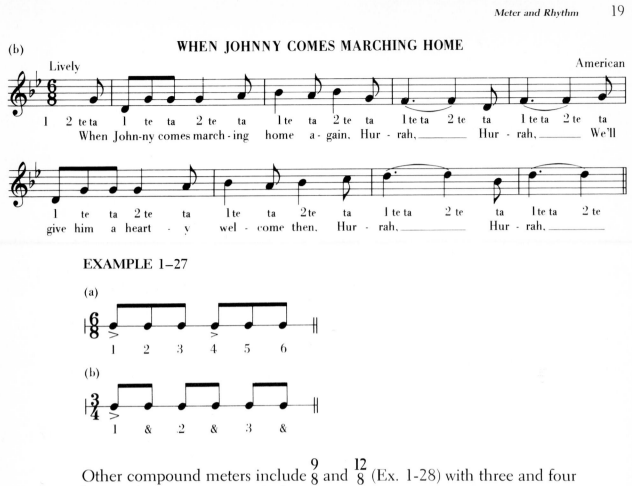

EXAMPLE 1–27

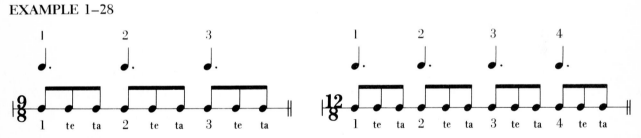

Other compound meters include $\frac{9}{8}$ and $\frac{12}{8}$ (Ex. 1-28) with three and four beats per measure, respectively.

EXAMPLE 1–28

◖ EXERCISE 1-7 Practice counting and clapping the following rhythms in compound meters $\frac{6}{8}$, $\frac{9}{8}$, and $\frac{12}{8}$.

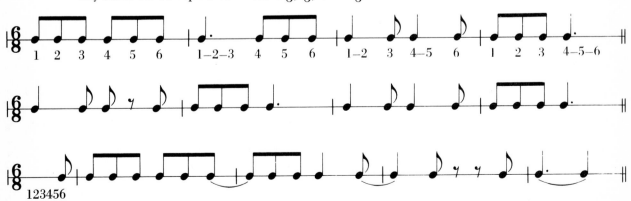

Perform the following rhythmic duets in compound meters. Have one individual or group perform the top line of each duet while a second individual or group performs the bottom line.

Beaming

Beams are often used instead of flags for notating two or more adjacent eighth, sixteenth, thirty-second, or sixty-fourth notes. Improper beaming, however, may obscure the location of the beats and confuse the performer. Example 1–29*a*, *b*, and *c* demonstrates how improper beaming may be corrected.

EXAMPLE 1–29

❰EXERCISE 1-8   Clarify each of the following rhythms by properly grouping and beaming notes. Check solutions in the left column.

Answers	Beaming notes

Triplets

A triplet, designated by a "3" or $\lceil$―3―$\rceil$ above or below the affected notes, indicates that triple division replaces duple division within the prevailing meter. Such a pattern may involve a single beat (Ex. 1-30*a*), a

EXAMPLE 1–30

(a)

(b)

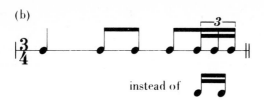

instead of

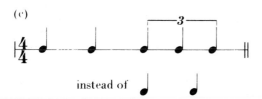

(c)

instead of

part of a beat (Ex. 1-30*b*), or more than one beat (Ex. 1-30*c*). In "Pilgrims' Chorus" in Example 1–31, for instance, triplets occur on single beats.

EXAMPLE 1–31

PILGRIMS' CHORUS

Richard Wagner

Syncopation

Any departure from the normal pattern of accents within an established meter is called *syncopation*. The anticipated pattern of accents on strong beats may be interrupted in a number of ways (Ex. 1-32*a* through *c*), or syncopation may occur within a beat (Ex. 1-32*d*).

EXAMPLE 1–32

a. Dynamic accents placed on beats that are normally unaccented

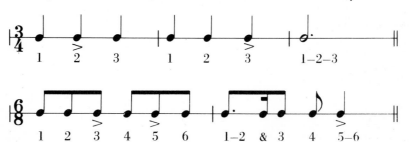

b. Duration on a weak beat connected to the succeeding strong beat

c. All or part of a strong beat eliminated with a rest

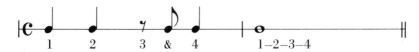

d. The procedures from (*a*), (*b*), and (*c*) above applied to single beats

Compare the syncopation in Example 1–32*b* with that in "Nobody Knows the Trouble I've Seen" in Example 1–33.

EXAMPLE 1–33

NOBODY KNOWS THE TROUBLE I'VE SEEN

Spiritual

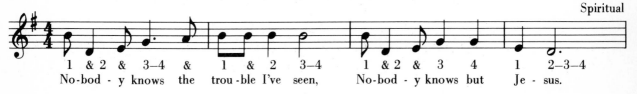

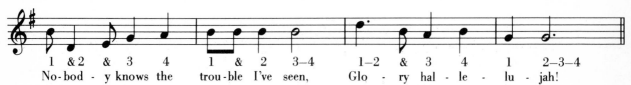

Asymmetrical Meters

Asymmetrical meters, such as $\frac{5}{4}$, $\frac{5}{8}$, $\frac{7}{4}$, and $\frac{7}{8}$, result from various combinations of accent patterns. In Example 1–34*a* and *b*, the accents reveal subgroups of three beats and two beats.

EXAMPLE 1–34

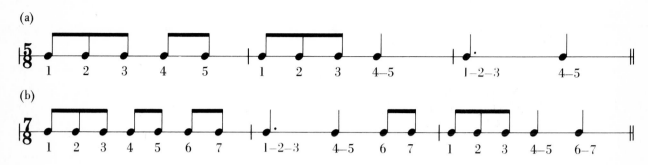

❰EXERCISE 1-9 Practice counting and clapping the following rhythms. Triplets, syncopation, and asymmetrical meters are included.

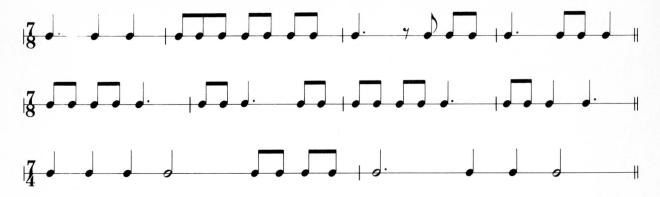

Reinforcing Meters with Texture

The grouping of accented beats is the chief means of establishing meter in a composition, but aspects such as *texture* contribute significantly. The word *texture*, which generally refers to the surface features or appearance of physical objects, is also useful for describing the look of a musical score (written notation). The texture of Chopin's *Waltz* for piano in Example 1–35 reveals a great deal about how he has reinforced the $\frac{3}{4}$ meter with his materials. The music on the lower staff, played by the pianist's left hand, serves as an accompaniment or background for the melodic line in the right hand. The left-hand pattern, a single note followed by two chords (vertically arranged notes played simultaneously), makes the three-beat grouping of $\frac{3}{4}$ meter not only visually apparent but audible in performance as well.

EXAMPLE 1–35

WALTZ

Moderato

Frédéric Chopin

As discussed earlier, a composition in a rapid tempo in $\frac{6}{8}$ meter is usually counted using two beats per measure. In Example 1–36, the placement of chords with longer durations (quarter notes and dotted quarter notes) emphasizes the two-beat pattern, indicated with arrows.

The texture of Haydn's string quartet (Ex. 1-37) reveals how the $\frac{4}{4}$ meter is reinforced. Although the melody in the first violin moves almost continually, the strong first and third beats of the $\frac{4}{4}$ meter are emphasized by the three lower instruments.

EXAMPLE 1–36

Ludwig van Beethoven

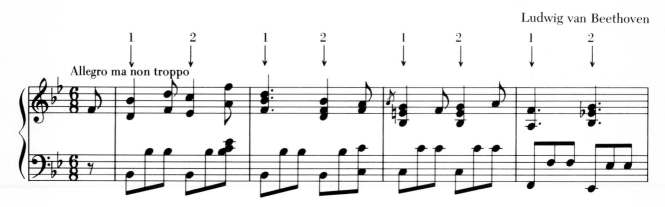

EXAMPLE 1–37

QUARTET No. 66

Franz Joseph Haydn

CHAPTER TWO

Notation of Pitch

The Musical Staff and the Treble and Bass Clefs

The notation of tones, or *pitches*, is essential for conveying the ideas of the composer to the performer. Pitches are traditionally notated on a five-line *staff* (Ex. 2-1). A special sign called a *clef* is used to assign letter names to the lines and spaces of the staff. Although there are several clefs, the *treble clef* and the *bass clef* are the most common. In Example 2-1*a*, the treble clef, or G clef, at the beginning of the staff designates the second line from the bottom as G. The treble clef is generally used for notating music for higher-pitched voices and instruments. In Example 2–1*b*, the bass clef, or F clef, establishes the fourth line from the bottom as F. This clef is used for notating music for lower-pitched voices and instruments.

EXAMPLE 2–1

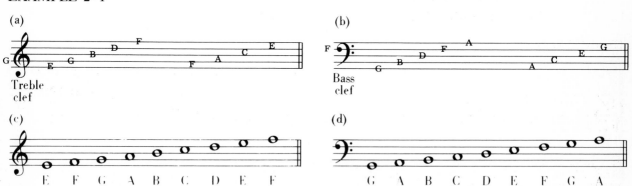

With the G line for the treble clef and the F line for the bass clef as starting points, the remaining lines and spaces are easily identified. Only the first seven letters of the alphabet (A–G) are used; after the pitch G, the series begins again with A. When noteheads are placed consecutively in ascending order on the staff, as in Example 2–1*c* and *d*, the alphabetical series of pitch names becomes apparent.

EXAMPLE 2–2

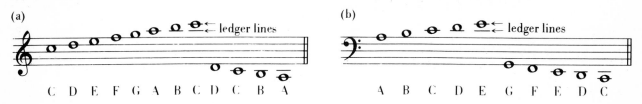

Pitches above or below the staff are notated by using *ledger lines*, as shown in Example 2–2*a* and *b*. When many ledger lines would be required to notate pitches above the staff, composers may instead write *8va*-------------or *8* ----------- above the notes, indicating that they are to be played an *octave* (eight tones) higher than written (Example 2-3*a*). The sign *8 bassa*--------- or *8* --------- is placed below notes to be played an octave lower than written (Ex. 2-3*b*). These octave signs provide a practical way of avoiding large numbers of ledger lines in more extreme ranges.

EXAMPLE 2–3

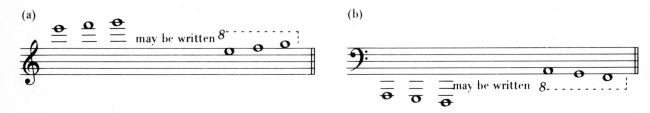

The Grand Staff

The *grand staff*, a treble staff and a bass staff connected with a bracket, is used to notate piano music and four-part chorales. Several octaves from the middle range of the piano are shown on the grand staff in Example 2–4. *Middle C*, located in the center of the keyboard, is written on a ledger line near either the treble or the bass staff.

EXAMPLE 2–4

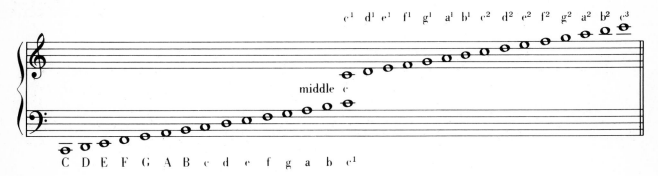

Notice in Example 2–4 that each pitch name is repeated every octave. On the grand staff, octaves are identified by a system of letters and numbers. All octaves from middle C upward (Ex. 2-5*a*) are identified with lowercase letters and superscripts: c^1, c^2, and so on. The octaves below middle C (Ex. 2-5*b*) use only lowercase or uppercase letters: c, C, CC, and so on.

EXAMPLE 2–5

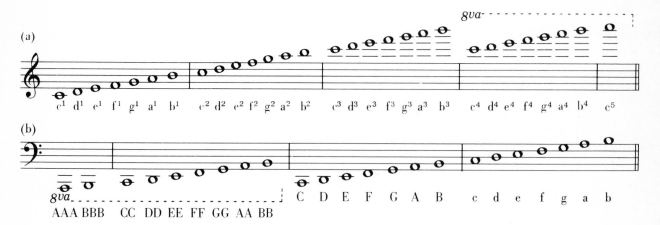

❰EXERCISE 2-1   After studying Examples 2–4 and 2–5, use the system of octave identification to name the pitches in the right column. Check answers in the left column.

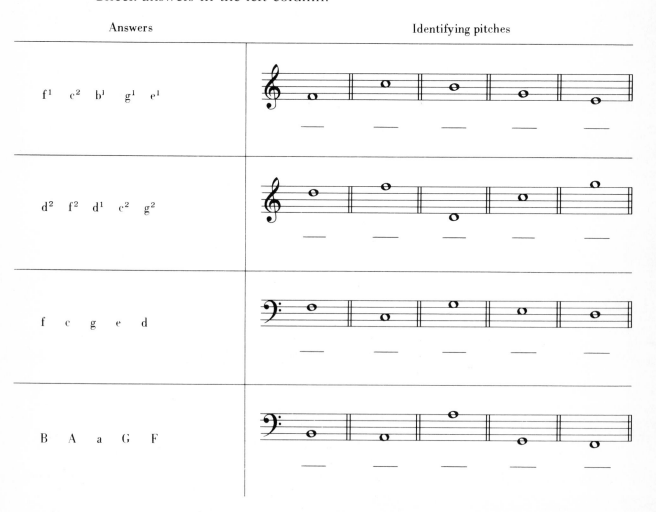

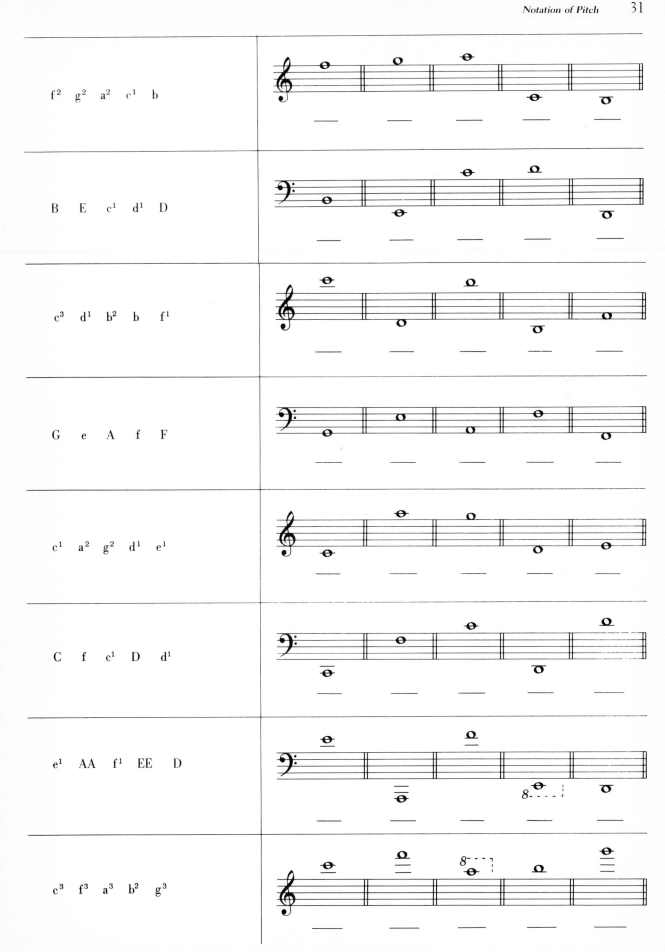

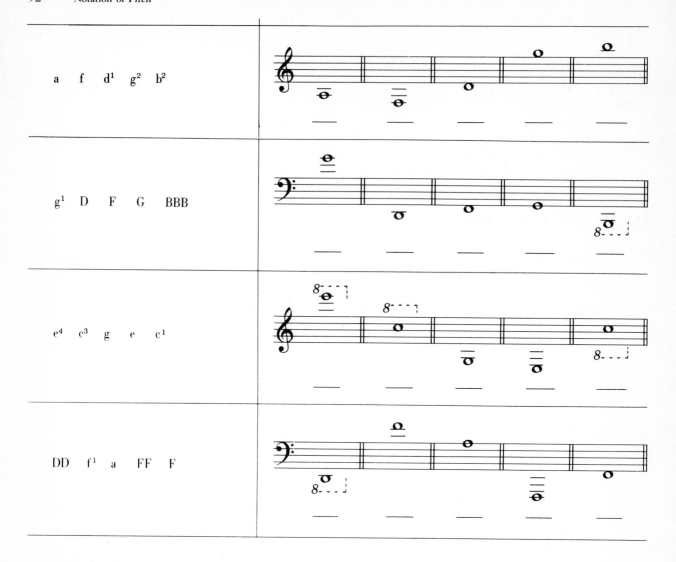

a	f	d¹	g²	b²

g¹	D	F	G	BBB

e⁴	c³	g	e	c¹

DD	f¹	a	FF	F

The C Clef

Certain instruments produce tones that lie within the lower range of the treble clef and the upper range of the bass clef. Neither of these clefs can accommodate the full range of those instruments without requiring numerous ledger lines. A way to alleviate this problem is to use the C *clef*, which reassigns the names of the lines and spaces. Unlike the treble and bass clefs, the C clef is movable. The line or space that falls within the center of the clef is designated as c¹, or middle C (Ex. 2-6). The two versions of the C clef used most frequently are the *tenor clef* and the *alto clef*. Although trombone parts are usually written in the bass clef, passages such as the second measure in Example 2–7a require many ledger lines.

EXAMPLE 2–6

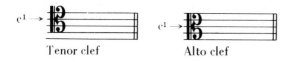

Tenor clef   Alto clef

EXAMPLE 2–7

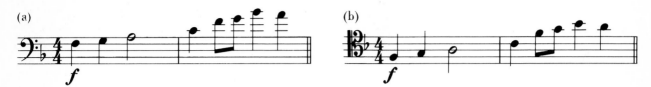

(a)

(b)

As shown in Example 2–7*b*, by using the tenor clef this second measure needs fewer ledger lines.

The Harmonic Series

The relative high or low quality of a pitch is determined by the frequency of vibrations. The more vibrations per second a tone has, the higher its pitch will be. A tuba, for instance, produces lower pitches having fewer vibrations per second than does a flute, whose tones lie in the higher pitch range and have more vibrations per second.

If a trombone, bassoon, and piano each play the tone notated in Example 2–8, the same pitch will result. Even when these three instru-

EXAMPLE 2–8

piano   bassoon   trombone

ments are playing the same pitch, however, you can tell that each instrument has its unique sound. In other words, a trombone sounds like a trombone and not like a piano or a bassoon. The unique sound or tone quality of each instrument is called its *timbre*, which is determined by a phenomenon known as the *harmonic series*. What may be surprising is that a single pitch consists of a fundamental vibration plus a mixture of weaker frequencies called *overtones*. When playing the lowest pitch in Example 2–9, all three of the instruments mentioned above would produce a series of overtones. The fundamental and the overtones produced from it are sometimes referred to as *partials*, the first eight of which are shown in Example 2–9. The physical characteristics of an instrument (size, shape, means of producing tone) affect the relative strength of its various overtones and thus its tone color or timbre.

EXAMPLE 2–9

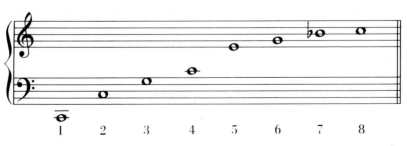

The Piano Keyboard

The piano keyboard serves as an excellent visual representation of the various relationships between tones. As may be seen in Example 2–10, the keys to the right are referred to as "up," and the keys to the left are "down." The tone G is higher than F, A is higher than G, and so on.

EXAMPLE 2–10

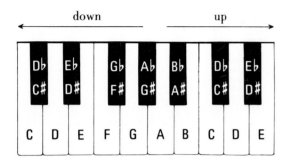

Half Steps and Whole Steps

Each black key is ½-step above or below an adjacent white key. For example, the black key to the right of G is G♯ (G-sharp), ½-step higher than G (Ex. 2–11). The same black key is also called A♭ (A-flat), ½-step lower than A. Because both the G♯ and the A♭ designate the same key on

EXAMPLE 2–11

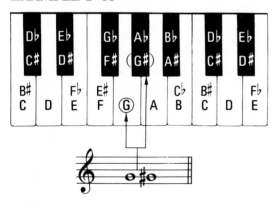

EXAMPLE 2–12

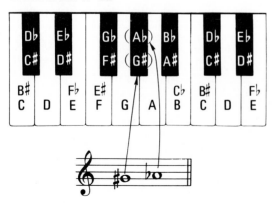

the keyboard, these two tones are known as *enharmonic tones* (Ex. 2-12). All other keys on the keyboard also have more than one letter name.

Notice that the white keys E and F, and B and C do not have black keys between them and are therefore only ½-step apart. All other adjacent white keys are a whole step apart. The pattern of whole (W) and half (H) steps between white keys is summarized in Example 2–13.

EXAMPLE 2–13

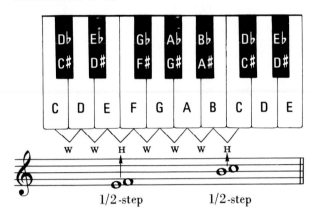

Accidentals (♯, ♭, ♮)

Accidentals are used to alter tones and in musical notation are always placed *before* the tone to be altered. A sharp (♯) raises a tone ½-step (Ex. 2-14a), while a flat (♭) lowers a tone ½-step (Ex. 2-14b). A natural (♮) cancels a ♯ or ♭ (Ex. 2-14c). A double sharp (𝄪) raises a tone two ½-steps; a double flat (♭♭) lowers a tone two ½-steps (Ex. 2-12d and e). The altering of tones by using accidentals is also known as *chromatic alteration*.

EXAMPLE 2–14

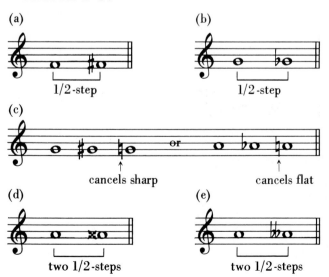

The Chromatic Scale

The *chromatic scale* contains all twelve tones within an octave in order by half steps. Traditionally, tones are altered with sharps in the ascending form (Ex. 2-15a) and flats in the descending form (Ex. 2-15b).

EXAMPLE 2–15

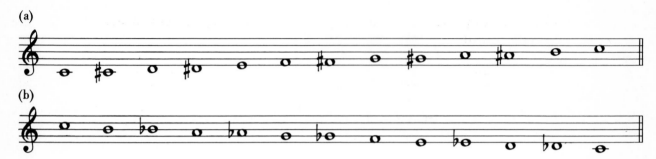

❰EXERCISE 2-2   Identify the pitches on the staves in the right column. Check answers in the left column.

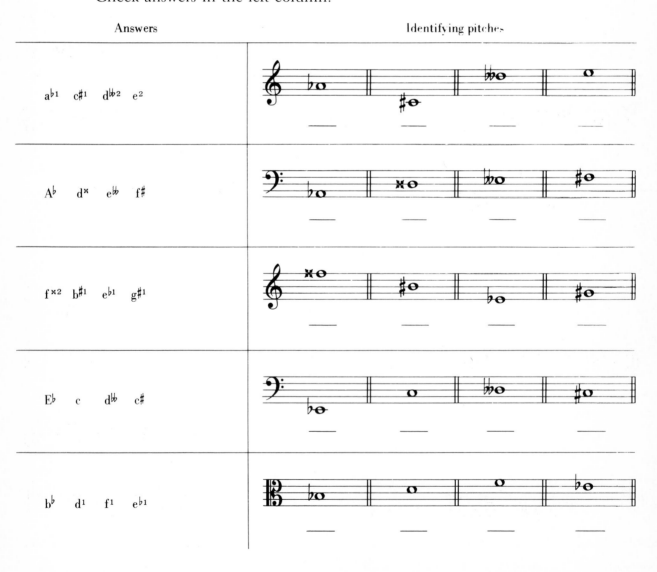

Answers

$a^{\flat 1}$ $c^{\sharp 1}$ $d^{\flat\flat 2}$ e^2

$A^\flat$ $d^\times$ $e^{\flat\flat}$ $f^\sharp$

$f^{\times 2}$ $b^{\sharp 1}$ $e^{\flat 1}$ $g^{\sharp 1}$

$E^\flat$ c $d^{\flat\flat}$ $c^\sharp$

$b^\flat$ d^1 f^1 $e^{\flat 1}$

Identifying pitches

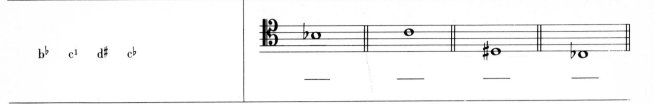

b♭   c¹   d♯   c♭

On the staves provided below, lower each pitch ½-step. Check answers in the left column.

Answers   Lowering pitches

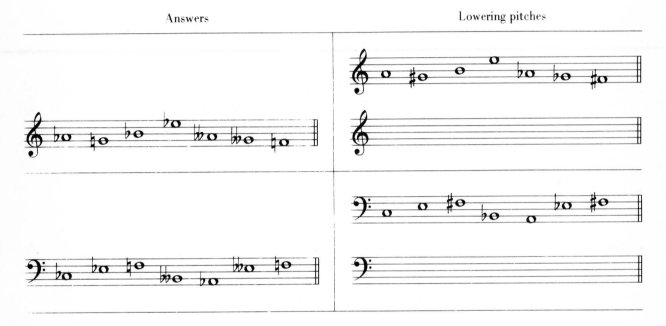

On the staves provided below, raise each pitch ½-step. Check answers in the left column.

Answers   Raising pitches

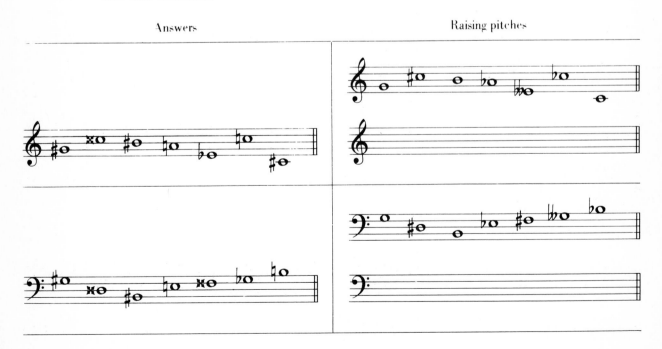

CHAPTER THREE
Introduction to Major Scales

The Major Scale in Three Common Keys

The tones in a composition may be arranged in an ascending or descending pattern known as a *scale*. Although there are many scales, the two most common patterns in Western music are the *major scale* and the *minor scale*. This chapter introduces only major scales; minor scales will be discussed in Chapter 7.

The *major scale* is a pattern of eight consecutive tones with half steps between the 3rd and 4th and the 7th and 8th degrees. As shown in Example 3–1*a*, the keyboard is a good visual aid for understanding these

EXAMPLE 3–1

(a)

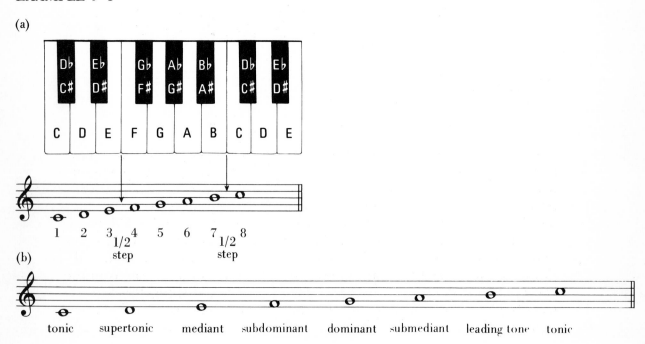

(b)

38

tonal relationships. Playing from C to C on the white keys only produces the *C-major scale*. In Example 3–1*b*, the names for the scale degrees are given under the tones.

If the major scale is moved to tonal levels other than C to C (e.g., F to F, or G to G), sharps or flats must be added to preserve the pattern of half steps between the 3rd and 4th and the 7th and 8th scale degrees. Between F and F on the white keys only of the keyboard, half steps fall between the 4th and 5th and the 7th and 8th degrees (Ex. 3-2*a*). To place

EXAMPLE 3–2

(a)

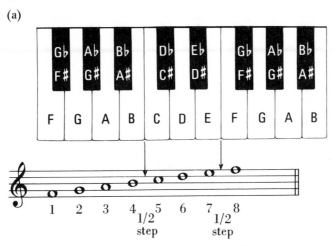

(b)

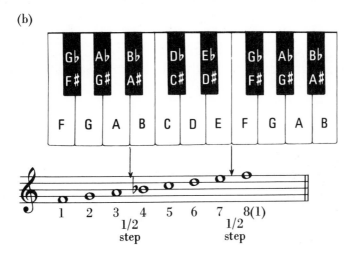

the necessary half step between the 3rd and 4th degrees, a B♭ (black note to the left of B) must be added (Ex. 3-2*b*). No other accidentals are necessary in the F major scale because the 7th and 8th degrees already have a half step between them. The major scale beginning on G (Ex. 3-3) requires an F♯ to produce the half step between its 7th and 8th degrees.

The 1st degree of a scale is the *tonal center*, or *key*. (The term *key* here should not be confused with a white or black key on the keyboard.) For example, a musical composition based on the F-major scale is in the key of F major. Sharps or flats necessary for establishing the key are usually placed on the staff after the clef, in an arrangement called a *key signature* (Ex. 3-4*b* and *c*). Remember that the key of C major (Ex. 3-4*a*)

EXAMPLE 3–3

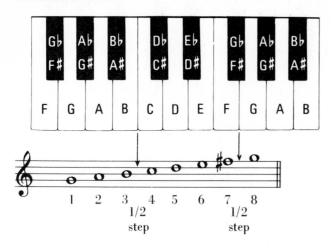

EXAMPLE 3–4

(a) C major

(b) F major

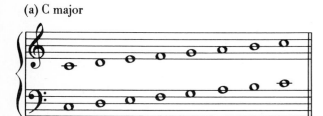

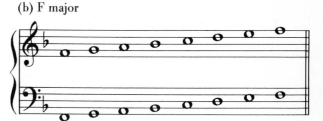

(c) G major

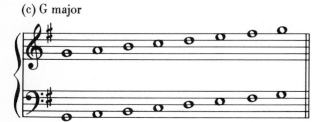

requires no sharps or flats. Unless indicated otherwise (by use of accidentals or a new key signature), the sharps or flats in the key signature remain in effect throughout a composition.

◖**EXERCISE 3-1**   After studying Example 3–4, practice writing the C-, F-, and G-major scales on the staves in the right column. Check written scales with answers in the left column.

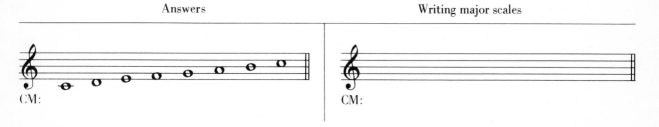

Answers   Writing major scales

CM: CM:

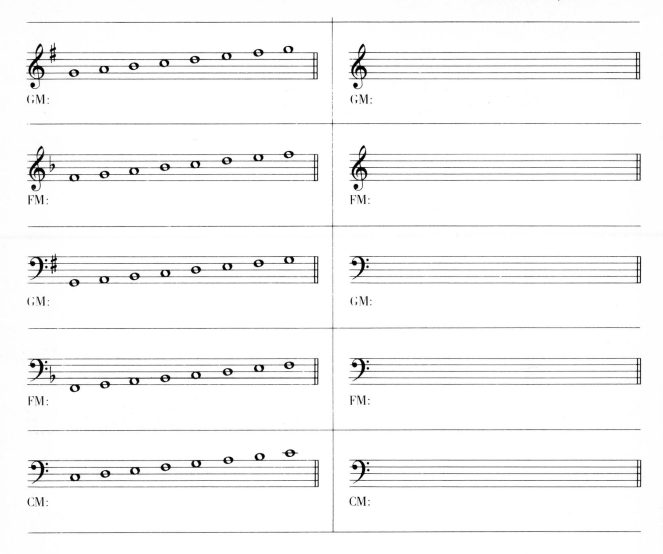

GM: GM:

FM: FM:

GM: GM:

FM: FM:

CM: CM:

Options for Further Study

Depending upon individual needs or course objectives, two options are open at this point. If desired, turn to Chapter 4, "Fundamentals of Melody," and learn about some of the basic processes in melody. The material in the first section of Chapter 4 is limited to the three major keys studied in this chapter. Or, continue with this chapter and study the remaining major keys.

The Remaining Major Keys

Keys with Sharps in Their Key Signatures

As explained in the first section of this chapter, the key of C major requires no sharps or flats in its key signature. To build a major scale on a tonal level other than C, however, sharps or flats are needed to maintain the pattern of half steps between the 3rd and 4th and the 7th and 8th scale

EXAMPLE 3–5

C major: 0 sharps

D major: 2 sharps

E major: 4 sharps

F♯ major: 6 sharps

G major: 1 sharp

A major: 3 sharps

B major: 5 sharps

C♯ major: 7 sharps

degrees. In Example 3–5, C major is included with G major and the remaining major keys that require sharps.

When the names of the sharp keys in Example 3–5 are arranged in an ascending stepwise order, as in Example 3–6, they resemble the C-major scale, except for the F♯ and C♯. Notice that the number of sharps in these keys falls into two sets—an ascending series of even numbers start-

EXAMPLE 3–6

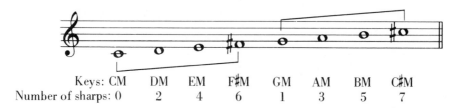

Keys:	CM	DM	EM	F♯M	GM	AM	BM	C♯M
Number of sharps:	0	2	4	6	1	3	5	7

ing on C major (0, 2, 4, 6), followed by ascending odd numbers starting on G major (1, 3, 5, 7). Use the odd- and even-number series in Example 3–6 to *memorize* the number of sharps in each key. The "M" after each key name is an abbreviation for "major." In later chapters, a lowercase letter (m) will be used as an abbreviation in minor key names.

Writing Scales in Sharp Keys

The names and order of the sharps in key signatures are revealed if you move the series of even and odd numbers back one place (Ex. 3-7). The first sharp in a key signature is always F♯, the second is C♯, the third G♯, and so on.

EXAMPLE 3–7

Keys:	C	D	E	F♯	G	A	B	C♯	
Number of sharps:	0	2	4	6	1	3	5	7	
Order of sharps:	2	4	6	1	3	5	7		← Moved back one place

You may write the scale of any sharp key by following three simple steps (see Box 3–1).

BOX 3–1

Problem: Write the scale of D major.
Step 1: Place the notes D to D on the staff.

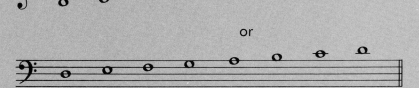

or

Step 2: Determine the number of sharps in the key of D major.

Keys:	C	D	E	F♯	G	A	B	C♯
Number of sharps:	0	②	4	6	1	3	5	7
Order of sharps:	2	4	6	1	3	5	7	

Answer: D major has two sharps

Step 3: Working from left to right, write the odd-numbered sharps ascending from F♯ and the even-numbered sharps ascending from C♯. (Because D major has two sharps, you will write one odd-numbered sharp and one even-numbered sharp.)

Keys:	C	D	E	F♯	G	A	B	C♯
Number of sharps:	0	②	4	6	1	3	5	7
Order of sharps:	2	4	6	1	3	5	7	

Answer:

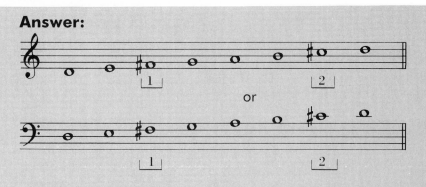

Problem: Write the scale of E major.
Step 1: Place the notes E to E on the staff.

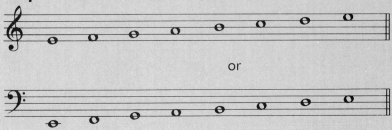

Step 2: Determine the number of sharps in the key of E major.

Keys:	C	D	E	F♯	G	A	B	C♯
Number of sharps:	0	2	④	6	1	3	5	7
Order of sharps:	2	4	6	1	3	5	7	

   Answer: E major has four sharps

Step 3: Working from left to right, write the odd-numbered sharps ascending from F♯ and the even-numbered sharps ascending from C♯. (Because E major has four sharps, you will write two odd-numbered sharps and two even-numbered sharps.)

Keys:	C	D	E	F♯	G	A	B	C♯
Number of sharps:	0	2	④	6	1	3	5	7
Order of sharps:	2	4	6	1	3	5	7	

Answer:

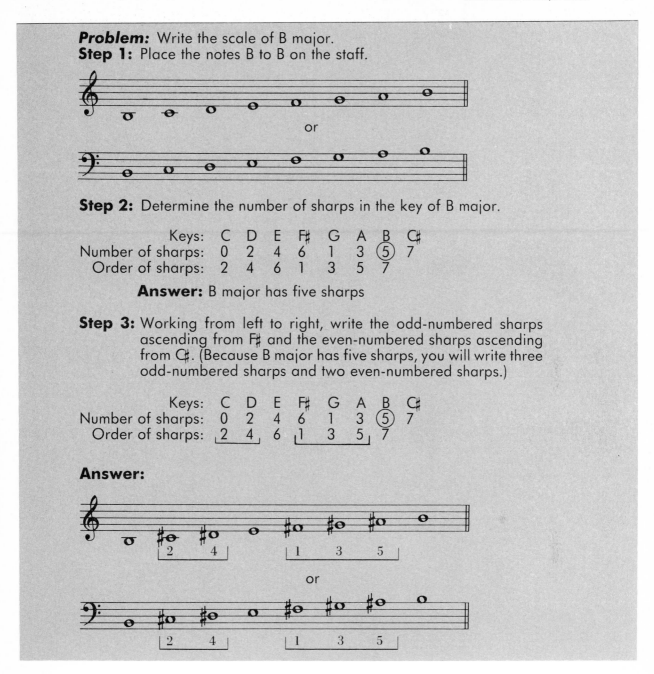

Problem: Write the scale of B major.
Step 1: Place the notes B to B on the staff.

or

Step 2: Determine the number of sharps in the key of B major.

Keys:	C	D	E	F♯	G	A	B	C♯
Number of sharps:	0	2	4	6	1	3	⑤	7
Order of sharps:	2	4	6	1	3	5	7	

Answer: B major has five sharps

Step 3: Working from left to right, write the odd-numbered sharps ascending from F♯ and the even-numbered sharps ascending from C♯. (Because B major has five sharps, you will write three odd-numbered sharps and two even-numbered sharps.)

Keys:	C	D	E	F♯	G	A	B	C♯
Number of sharps:	0	2	4	6	1	3	⑤	7
Order of sharps:	2	4	6	1	3	5	7	

Answer:

or

❰EXERCISE 3-2 Practice writing scales of sharp keys in the right column. Check written scales with answers in the left column.

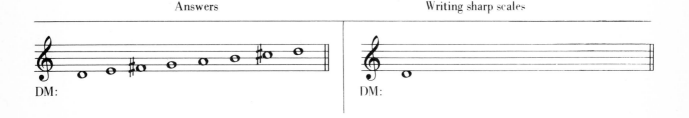

Answers

Writing sharp scales

DM:

DM:

EM:

EM:

CM:

CM:

AM:

AM:

F#M:

F#M:

GM:

GM:

GM:

GM:

DM:

DM:

C#M:

C#M:

BM:

BM:

Writing Key Signatures for Sharp Keys

As described in the previous section, sharps in a key signature are written in a particular order (Ex. 3-8). Notice that the order of the sharps alter-

EXAMPLE 3–8

Keys:	C	D	E	F♯	G	A	B	C♯
Number of sharps:	0	2	4	6	1	3	5	7
Order of sharps:	2	4	6	1	3	5	7	

even   odd

EXAMPLE 3–9

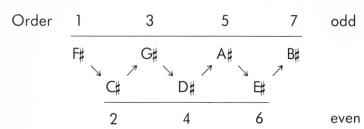

Order   1   3   5   7   odd

F#   G#   A#   B#

C#   D#   E#

2   4   6   even

nates between the odd and even brackets, resulting in the arrangement in Example 3–9. When sharps are placed in key signatures on the staff (Ex. 3-10*a* and *b*), F# is first, C# second, G# third, and so on.

EXAMPLE 3–10

(a)

1   2   3   4   5   6   7

F#   C#   G#   D#   A#   E#   B#

(b)

EXAMPLE 3–11

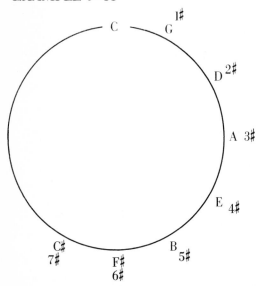

The relationship between keys is traditionally displayed in the *circle of fifths*. In the partial circle of fifths in Example 3–11, only C major and the sharp keys are given. Each sharp key to the right (clockwise) of C major is five tones higher and has one more sharp than the previous key. For example, the key of G major has one sharp, D major has two sharps, and so on. The remainder of the circle will be completed after flat keys are studied later in this chapter.

◖**EXERCISE 3-3**   Practice writing key signatures for sharp keys in the right column. Check answers in the left column.

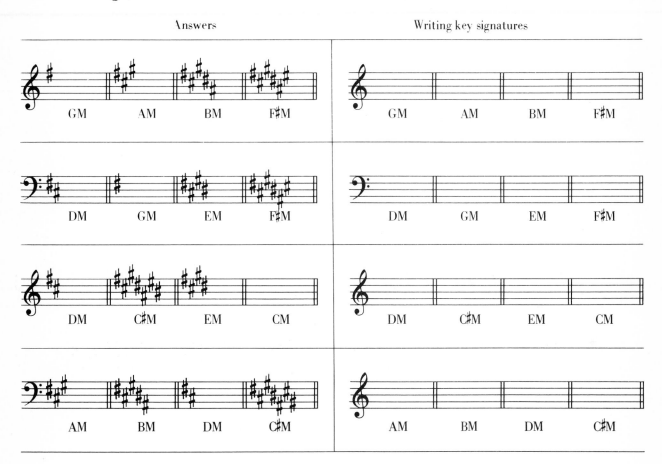

Keys with Flats in Their Key Signatures

F major and the remaining flat keys are shown in Example 3–12. (Except for F major, all the flat keys have the flat sign in their names, e.g., B♭, E♭, and A♭.) The key of C major (no sharps or flats), which was included with the sharp keys, is also included with this group. A system of odd and even numbers may also be used to determine the number of flats in a key. However, as shown in Example 3–13, the numbers are in the reverse order of those for the sharp keys. Notice that the number of sharps and flats for any two keys with the same letter names (e.g., C and C♭) always equals seven. If you know that G major has one sharp in its key signature, you can calculate that G-flat major has six flats, or the difference between one and seven. Since A major has three sharps in its key signature, then A-flat major has four flats. Before proceeding further, *memorize* the number of flats in each key.

EXAMPLE 3–12

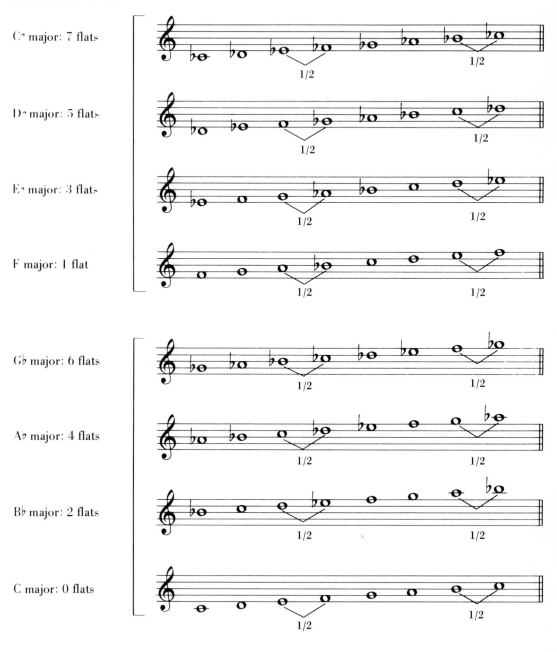

EXAMPLE 3–13

Sharp keys:	C	D	E	F♯	G	A	B	C♯
Number of sharps:	0	2	4	6	1	3	5	7

Flat keys:	C♭	D♭	E♭	F	G♭	A♭	B♭	C
Number of flats:	7	5	3	1	6	4	2	0

Writing Scales in Flat Keys

The names and order of flats in key signatures are summarized in Example 3–14; B♭ is the first flat in all key signatures of flat keys and thus the first of the odd-numbered series, while E♭ is the second flat and begins the even-numbered series.

EXAMPLE 3–14

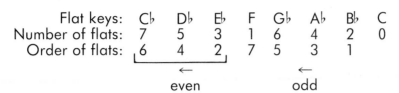

Flat keys:	C♭	D♭	E♭	F	G♭	A♭	B♭	C
Number of flats:	7	5	3	1	6	4	2	0
Order of flats:	6	4	2	7	5	3	1	

           ←   ←

        even   odd

Any scale with flats can be written by following steps similar to those used in writing sharp scales, as is shown in Box 3–2. (*Note:* When using the odd and even series to find the order of flats, work from *right* to *left*.)

BOX 3–2

Problem: Write the scale of A-flat major.
Step 1: Write the notes A to A on the staff.

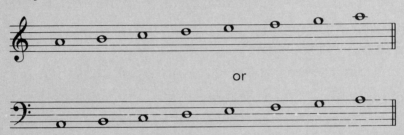

or

Step 2: Determine the number of flats in the key of A-flat major.

Keys:	C♭	D♭	E♭	F	G♭	A♭	B♭	C
Number of flats:	7	5	3	1	6	④	2	0
Order of flats:	6	4	2	7	5	3	1	

Answer: A-flat major has four flats

Step 3: Working from right to left, write the odd-numbered flats descending from B♭ and the even-numbered flats descending from E♭. (Because A-flat major has four flats, you will write two odd-numbered flats and two even-numbered flats.)

Keys:	C♭	D♭	E♭	F	G♭	A♭	B♭	C
Number of flats:	7	5	3	1	6	④	2	0
Order of flats:	6	4	2	7	5	3	1	

           ←   ←

Answer:

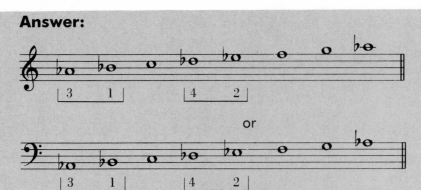

Problem: Write the scale of D-flat major.
Step 1: Write the notes D to D on the staff.

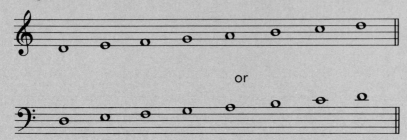

Step 2: Determine the number of flats in the key of D-flat major.

Keys:	C♭	D♭	E♭	F	G♭	A♭	B♭	C
Number of flats:	7	⑤	3	1	6	4	2	0
Order of flats:	6	4	2	7	5	3	1	

Answer: D-flat major has five flats

Step 3: Working from right to left, write the odd-numbered flats descending from B♭ and the even-numbered flats descending from E♭. (Because D-flat major has five flats, you will write three odd-numbered flats and two even-numbered flats.)

Keys:	C♭	D♭	E♭	F	G♭	A♭	B♭	C
Number of flats:	7	⑤	3	1	6	4	2	0
Order of flats:	6	4	2	7	5	3	1	

Answer:

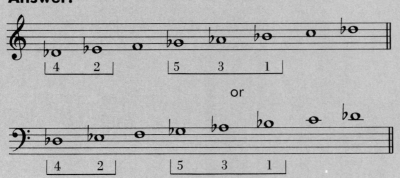

◀EXERCISE 3-4 Practice writing scales of flat keys in the right column. Check written scales with answers in the left column.

Answers | Writing flat scales

FM:

B♭M:

E♭M:

D♭M:

A♭M:

FM:

B♭M:

C♭M:

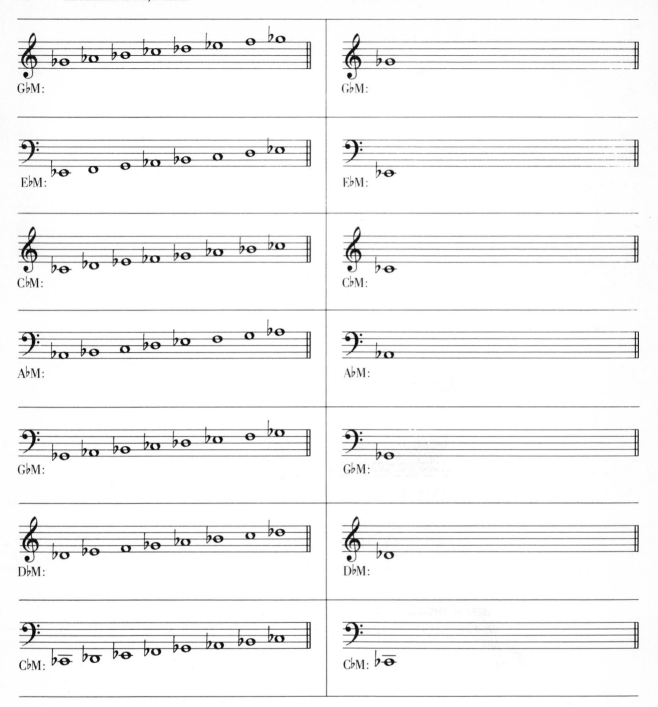

Writing Key Signatures for Flat Keys

Like sharps, flats are written in a particular order in a key signature (Ex. 3-15). Again, C major, which has no flats, is included in the series. The order of the flats alternates between the odd and even brackets, as in Example 3–16.

When flats are placed in a key signature on the staff (Ex. 3-17*a* and *b*), B♭ is first, E♭ second, A♭ third, and so on.

EXAMPLE 3–15

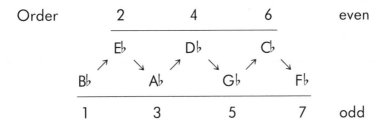

Keys:	Cb	Db	Eb	F	Gb	Ab	Bb	C
Number of flats:	7	5	3	1	6	4	2	0
Order of flats:	6	4	2	7	5	3	1	

EXAMPLE 3–16

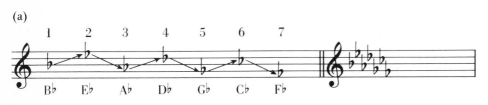

Order	2	4	6	even
	Eb	Db	Cb	
Bb	Ab	Gb	Fb	
1	3	5	7	odd

EXAMPLE 3–17

(a)

1   2   3   4   5   6   7

Bb   Eb   Ab   Db   Gb   Cb   Fb

(b)

Circle of Fifths

All sharp and flat keys are displayed in the circle of fifths in Example 3–18. As each sharp key to the right of C major is five tones higher than the previous key, each flat key to the left of C major is five tones lower. The key of F major, with one flat, is five tones lower than C major; the key of B-flat major, with two flats, is five tones lower than F major; and so on. Notice that in a portion near the lower side of the circle, three sharp and flat keys overlap. Recall from Chapter 2 that tones such as Db and C♯, which are the same key on the keyboard, are called *enharmonic tones*.

EXAMPLE 3–18

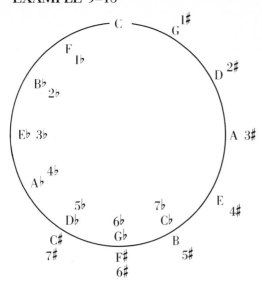

The scales of D-flat major and C-sharp major are spelled differently but involve the same black and white keys on the keyboard. The same is true of the other two pairs. Although this overlap could be carried further, the resulting keys are impractical. The key of F-flat is theoretically possible, but the eight flats make it unnecessarily difficult. The key of E major, the enharmonic equivalent of F-flat, contains only four sharps and is a very common key.

◀EXERCISE 3-5   Practice writing key signatures for flat keys in the right column. Check answers in the left column.

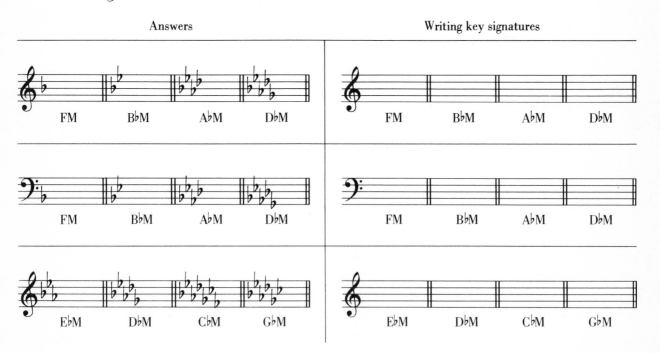

E♭M   D♭M   C♭M   G♭M

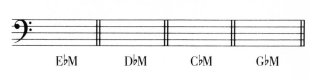

E♭M   D♭M   C♭M   G♭M

CHAPTER FOUR
Fundamentals of Melody

Basic Triad Outlines

Many simple melodies are based on the 1st, 3rd, and 5th scale degrees. Examples 4–1 through 4–6 help illustrate this relationship between *scale* and *melody* in the keys of C major, F major, and G major, respectively. On staff *a* of Examples 4–1, 4–3, and 4–5, the major scale is numbered 1 through 8; the 1st, 3rd, and 5th scale degrees are outlined on staff *b*. Collectively, the 1st, 3rd, and 5th scale degrees are known as the *tonic triad*, written vertically, or harmonically, on staff *c*. In a musical composition, notes written in harmonic form are intended to be sounded simultaneously. (More information about the tonic triad is available in Chapter 8.)

EXAMPLE 4–1

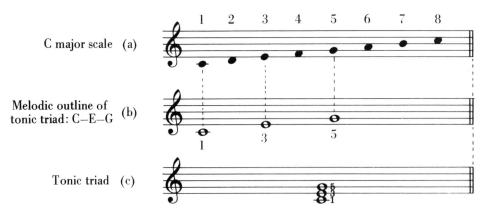

The tones on staff *b* in Examples 4–1, 4–3, and 4–5 are a "melodic outline" of the tonic triad and are sounded one at a time, reading from left to right. Because some of the simplest melodies consist of little more than outlines of the tonic triad, this important pattern is one of the fundamentals of melody (Exs. 4-2, 4-4, and 4-6).

58

EXAMPLE 4-2

OH, SUSANNA

Stephen C. Foster

EXAMPLE 4-3

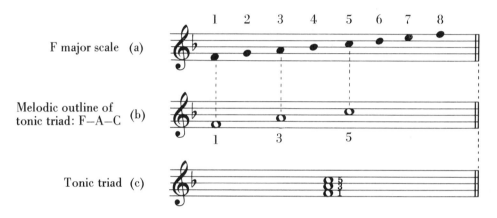

EXAMPLE 4-4

MICHAEL, ROW THE BOAT ASHORE

Spiritual

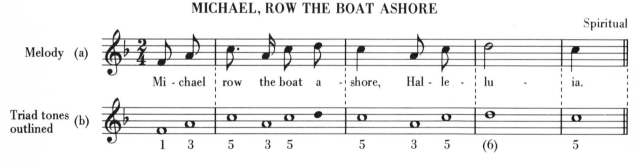

EXAMPLE 4-5

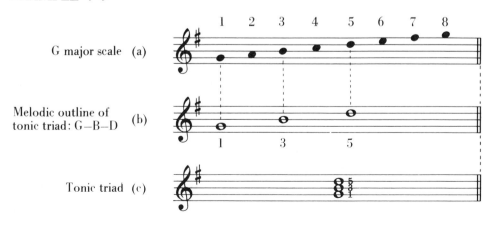

EXAMPLE 4–6

To emphasize the melodic structure of Examples 4–2, 4–4, and 4–6, pitch reductions are placed on the lower staves. Stripped of rhythmic considerations, the "whole notes" represent tones of the tonic triad. Other scale degrees, indicated with unstemmed black noteheads, will be discussed later under "Simple Melodic Embellishments." The pitch reductions reveal that these melodic fragments consist almost entirely of outlines of the tonic triad.

Dynamics

You will recall from Chapter 1 that tempo markings (e.g., *Largo*, *Moderato*, and *Allegro*) are used to indicate the speed at which compositions are to be performed. Throughout this book, you will also find *dynamic markings*, which indicate the level of volume or loudness for performing music. The most common dynamic markings are the following symbols and abbreviations of Italian words:

Symbol	Term	Definition
pp	pianissimo	very soft
p	piano	soft
mp	mezzopiano	moderately soft
mf	mezzoforte	moderately loud
f	forte	loud
ff	fortissimo	very loud
◁	crescendo	gradual increase in volume
▷	decrescendo	gradual decrease in volume
dim.	diminuendo	gradual decrease in volume

Phrase Markings and Other Symbols

Melodies often have curved lines ⌒ called phrase markings that indicate the logical grouping of tones. Performers find these markings useful for interpreting melodic lines.

Other common terms and symbols are as follows:

Symbol	Term	Definition
𝄐	fermata	Hold longer than the established value
𝄆 ⋮ 𝄇	repeat	Repeat material between the signs
⌐1.⌐ ⌐2.⌐ ⋮	endings	After the repeat, take ⌐2.⎯ instead of ⌐1.⎯
D.S. *al Fine*	*Dal Segno al Fine*	Repeat from the 𝄋 and end at *Fine*. (*Fine* means end)
D.C. *al Fine*	*Da Capo al Fine*	Repeat from the beginning of the piece and end at *Fine*

ℭEXERCISE 4-1   The following melodies are limited to outlines of the tonic triad in the keys of C major, F major, and G major. If necessary, review rhythm and meter in Chapter 1.

Suggested study:
1. Label tones in the melody as 1, 3, or 5 of the tonic triad.
2. Sing the triad outline on staff *b*.
3. Observing the meter, sing or clap the rhythm on staff *a*.
4. Sing the melody or play it on an instrument.

Wolfgang Amadeus Mozart

Analyze and sing the following melodies:

Simple Melodic Embellishments

Few melodies are limited to triad outlines exclusively; most have decorating tones that embellish those outlines. One such fundamental melodic embellishment is the *passing tone* (PT), which "passes" between tones in triad outlines. In Example 4–7, passing tones are indicated by the black noteheads on staff *b*. At "X," two passing tones are needed to fill the space between the 5th and 8th scale degrees.

EXAMPLE 4–7

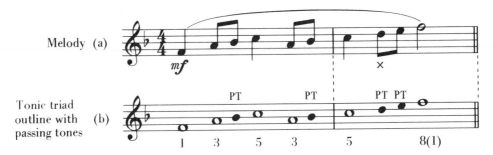

Another fundamental melodic embellishment is the *neighbor tone*. While the passing tone lies between two tones of *different* pitch, the neighbor tone occurs between two tones of the *same* pitch. In this way, a single pitch can be embellished by its *upper neighbor* (UN) or *lower neighbor* (LN) tone, as in Example 4–8.

EXAMPLE 4–8

The neighbor tone is particularly useful for adding rhythmic vitality to melodies by embellishing tones of the same pitch. In Example 4–9*a*, the tone G at "X" is prolonged simply by being repeated. On staff *b*, the sound of the underlying tone G remains prominent but is enhanced by its embellishing upper neighbor tone (UN).

EXAMPLE 4–9

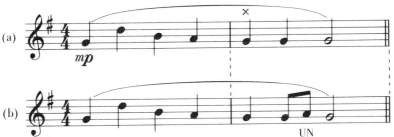

EXAMPLE 4–10

The potential of the neighbor tone in melodic variation is evident in Example 4–10. In the variation, the neighbor tones give more rhythmic interest to the "skeleton" theme.

Many melodies, regardless of how complex they may seem on the surface, consist primarily of triad tones, passing tones, and neighbor tones. Knowledge of these fundamentals of melody will be indispensable in the later chapters on improvising and harmonizing. Embellishing tones in melodic variations will be discussed more fully in Chapter 5.

✿EXERCISE 4-2   The melodies in this section contain tonic triad tones, passing tones, and neighbor tones. Space for triad analysis is provided below each melody. In the analysis of the first three melodies, the white noteheads on the lower staff represent tonic tones, while the black noteheads signify passing tones and neighbor tones.

Suggested study:

1. On the lower staff, use white and black noteheads to analyze the melody. Label passing tones (PT) and neighbor tones (UN or LN).
2. Sing or clap the rhythm.
3. Sing the melody or play it on an instrument.

Johannes Brahms

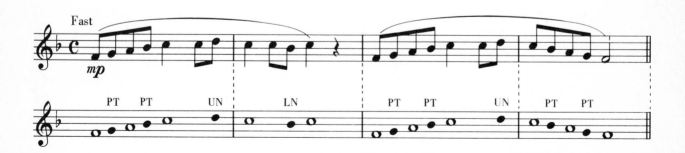

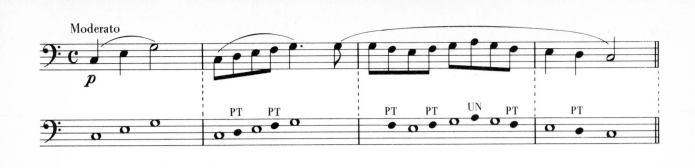

Johannes Brahms

Other Arrangements of the Tonic Triad Outline

Melodies in the previous sections of this chapter were based on outlines of the tonic triad with the 1st scale degree as the lowest tone (1–3–5). The melody in Example 4–11 outlines the tonic triad in a descending pattern

EXAMPLE 4–11

EXAMPLE 4–12

Franz Joseph Haydn

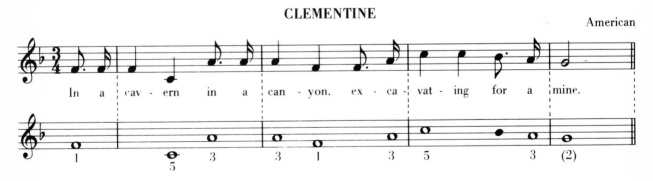

(5–3–1). In Example 4–12, the 5th scale degree is the lowest tone in the melody.

EXAMPLE 4–13

CLEMENTINE

American

In a cav-ern in a can-yon, ex-ca-vat-ing for a mine.

◀ EXERCISE 4-3 The following melodies contain various tonic triad outlines.

Suggested study:
1. On the lower staff, use white and black noteheads to analyze the melody. Label passing tones (PT) and neighbor tones (UN or LN).
2. Sing or clap the rhythm.
3. Sing the melody or play it on an instrument.

GOODNIGHT LADIES

Traditional

Good-night la-dies,   Good-night la-dies,   Good-night   la-dies we're going to leave you now.

Moderato

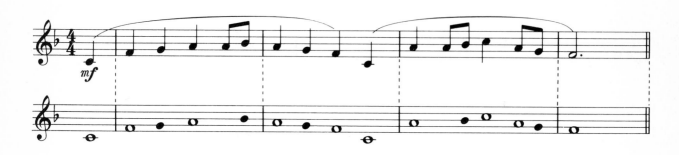

Ludwig van Beethoven

Presto

Andante

Underlying Scale Patterns

Analysis of highly embellished melodies often reveals simple underlying scalewise patterns similar to those in Examples 4–14 and 4–15.

EXAMPLE 4–14

EXAMPLE 4–15

◀EXERCISE 4-4   Using Examples 4–14 and 4–15 as guides, notate the scalewise motion of the following melodies on the staff provided below.

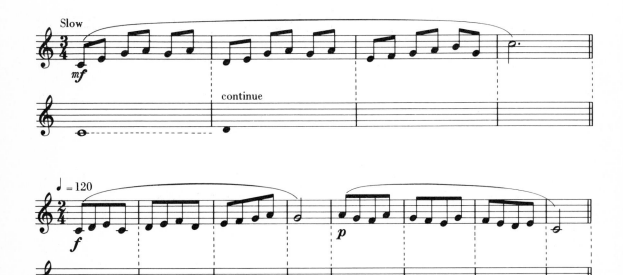

Analyze and sing the following familiar melodies. Look for triad outlines, embellishing tones, and scalewise motion.

MATCHMAKER
from the musical "Fiddler on the Roof"

Words by Sheldon Harnick

Music by Jerry Bock

Match-mak-er, match-mak-er, make me a match, Find me a find,

catch me a catch; Match-mak-er, match-mak-er, look through your book And

make me a per- fect match. Match-mak-er, match-mak-er,

I'll bring the veil, you bring the groom, slen-der and pale; Bring me a

ring, for I'm long-ing to be the en-vy of all I see._____

THEY CALL THE WIND MARIA

Words by Alan Jay Lerner

Music by Frederick Loewe

Options for Further Study

The remainder of this chapter includes melodies in additional keys. You may choose to study these melodies or proceed to Chapter 5, "Melodic Variation and Improvisation Techniques: An Introduction to Composing Music."

◗ **EXERCISE 4-5**   Using the methods outlined in this chapter, analyze and perform the following melodies.

THE ASH GROVE

Welsh

CHAPTER FIVE
Melodic Variation and Improvisation Techniques
An Introduction to Composing Music

The success of variation technique in music is apparent from its long history and widespread applications. One of the most significant applications of improvised or spontaneous variation in the twentieth century occurs in the solos of jazz performers, and in folk music, improvised variation continues to be a standard practice. Many composers have written sets of variations, and some have been known for their improvising skills as well. Regardless of whether melodic variation is improvised or written out in musical notation, the techniques involved require knowledge of the fundamentals of melody.

Melodic variation remains a common technique for composing music. One approach is to state a simple melody, or *theme*, and then repeat it a number of times with various changes. Ideally, variations that are endowed with the interest and surprise of new material will at the same time retain recognizable connections with the theme.

Analyzing Themes with Variations

Themes may be varied by adding melodic embellishments. Example 5–1 exhibits a few possibilities for the melodic variation of a simple melody (theme). In variations 1, 2, and 3, the theme is elaborated with passing tones (PT) and neighbor tones (UN, LN). Notice that when embellishing tones are added in the variations, the rhythm must also change to fit the meter.

In Mozart's theme and variations in Example 5–2, compare the first four measures of the theme with the corresponding portions of variations 1 and 2. Although at first glance the variations may not resemble the theme, closer analysis reveals that many of the tones of the original melody are present in the embellished versions.

EXAMPLE 5–1

Theme

Variation 1 (varied with upper neighbor tones (UN))

Variation 2 (varied with lower neighbor tones (LN))

Variation 3 (varied with neighbor tones and passing tones)

EXAMPLE 5–2

Theme

SONATA

Wolfgang Amadeus Mozart

Andante grazioso

Variation 1

Variation 2

❰**EXERCISE 5-1** The following themes are limited to the keys of C major, G major, and F major. In themes 1 through 3 circle all triad tones and in each variation label the embellishing tones (PT, UN, LN). Remember that the variations require rhythmic changes to accommodate embellishing tones.

1. Theme

Variation 1

Variation 2

Variation 3

Writing Variations on Themes

Writing variations on a theme provides an outlet for creative expression while at the same time offering the security of a given model. In this section, each melodic variation will involve changes in embellishing tones and rhythm. Additional variation techniques will be discussed in Chapter 12.

❰EXERCISE 5-2   Using the previous examples as guides, write variations for the following themes. Remember to make rhythmic changes wherever needed.

1. Theme

Variation 1

Variation 2

Variation 3

2. Theme

Variation 1

Variation 2

Variation 3

3. Theme

Variation 1

Variation 2

Variation 3

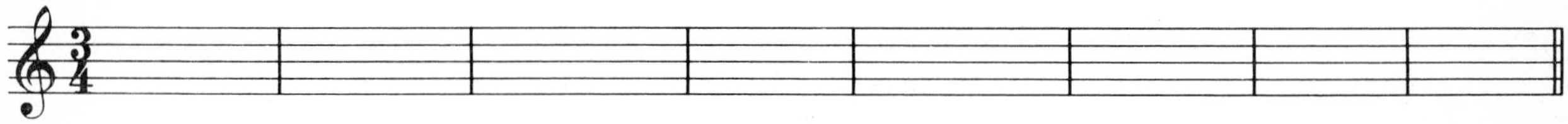

4. Theme

Slow

Variation 1

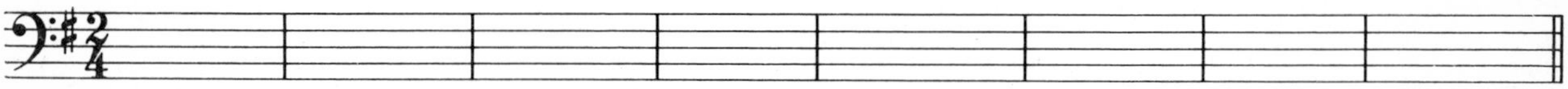

Variation 2

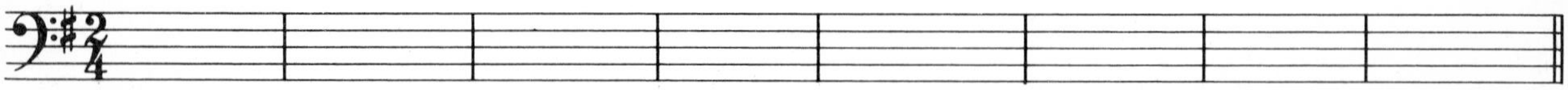

Variation 3

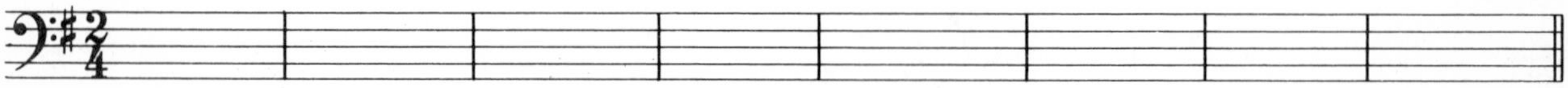

5. Theme

Variation 1

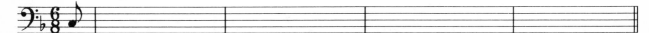

Variation 2

Variation 3

Options for Further Study

Depending upon individual needs or course objectives, two options are open at this point. You may turn to Chapter 6 and study intervals, or you may continue with the material in this chapter. The remainder of this chapter involves improvisation on simple melodies and variations on themes in additional keys.

Improvisation

If you play an instrument or sing, you may wish to *improvise,* or perform extemporaneously, your own simple variations on the themes in Exercise 5-2. When improvising for the first time, add only one or two embellishments. Become comfortable with the feel and sound of one improvised variation before attempting others. The following suggestions may be helpful:

1. Perform the melody without any alterations.
2. Perform a variation with only one or two passing tones or neighbor tones.
3. As you become more confident, experiment with more embellishments and different rhythm patterns.

Variations in Additional Keys

The remainder of this chapter contains themes in additional keys for more practice in writing variations.

◀ **EXERCISE 5-3**   Write or perform variations on the following themes. If necessary, refer to Chapter 3, "Introduction to Major Scales."

1. Theme

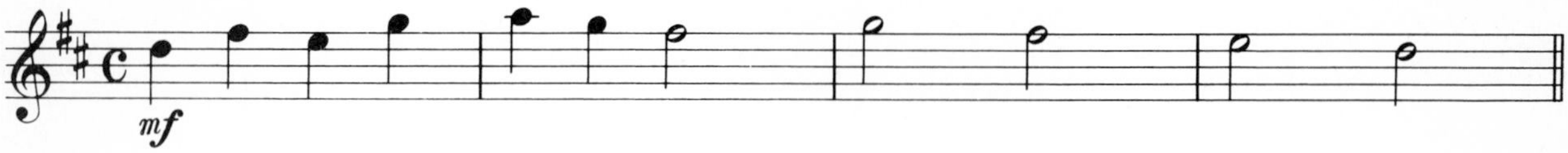

Variation 1

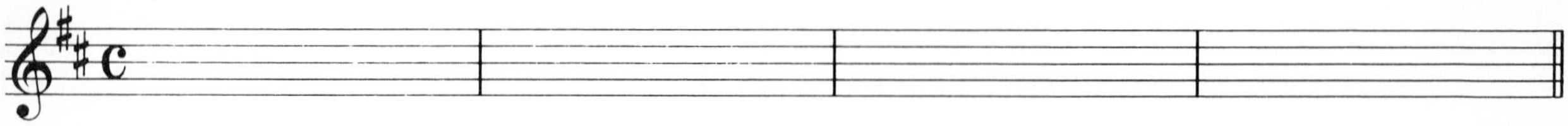

Variation 2

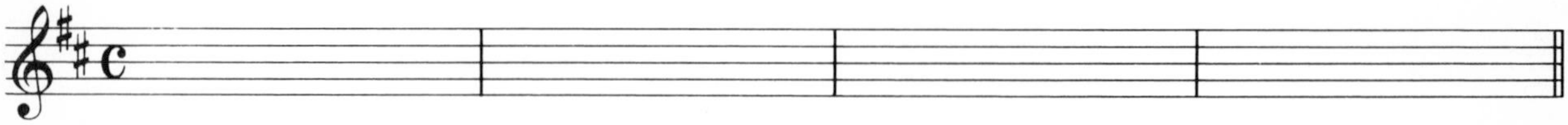

Variation 3

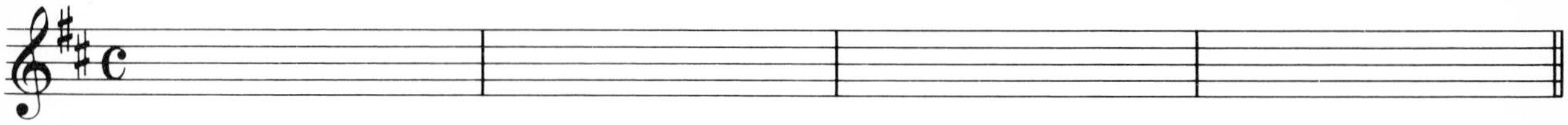

2. Theme

Variation 1

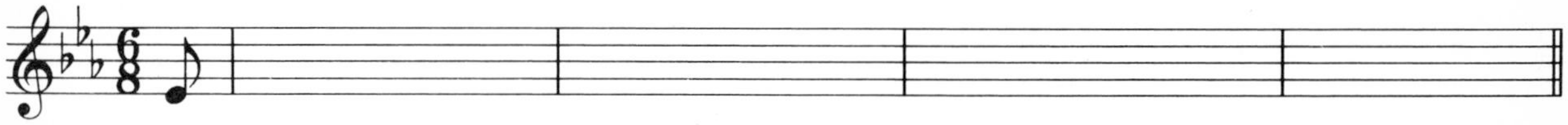

Variation 2

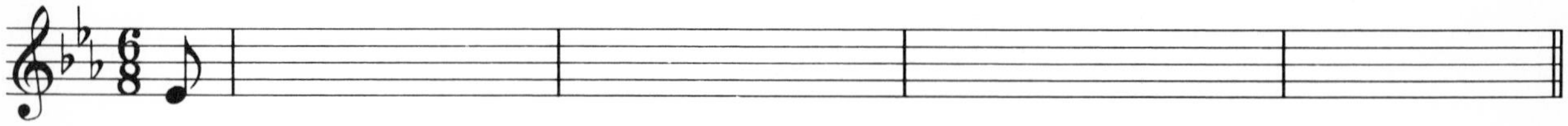

Variation 3

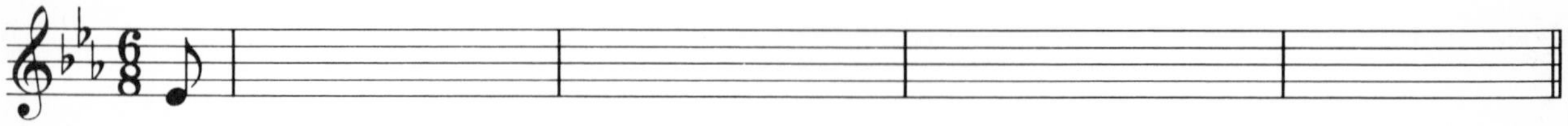

3. Theme

Variation 1

Variation 2

Variation 3

4. Theme

Variation 1

Variation 2

Variation 3

5. Theme

Variation 1

Variation 2

Variation 3

CHAPTER SIX
Intervals

An *interval* is the distance separating any two pitches. In general, starting with the upper or lower tone as *1*, an interval may be determined by counting the lines and spaces to and including the second tone. Notice in Example 6–1 that the tones of an interval may be stated harmonically (simultaneously), or melodically (one at a time). Although the numerical designation of intervals is necessary, it does not identify interval *quality*.

EXAMPLE 6–1

5th   6th   4th   2nd

The intervals in Example 6–2 are both 3rds but do not have the same quality. The first 3rd (C to E) contains four half steps and is a *major 3rd*, while the second 3rd (D to F) involves only three half steps and is a *minor 3rd*. As can be seen in many of the examples in this chapter, the keyboard provides an excellent visual aid for counting half steps and thus determining interval qualities.

EXAMPLE 6–2

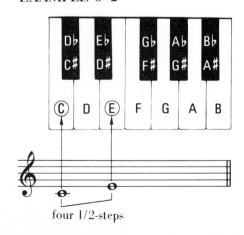
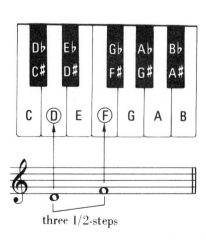

four 1/2-steps   three 1/2-steps

Each of the boxes in this chapter is devoted to a particular set of intervals. Before any accidentals are introduced, each box displays those intervals as found on the white keys only of the keyboard. For example, the first section of Box 6–1 gives all of the major 3rds and minor 6ths on the white keys only. Notice that when major 3rds are *inverted,* or turned upside down, they become minor 6ths.

The later sections of each box demonstrate the effects of accidentals on interval quality. When like accidentals are added to both pitches, the interval quality is unchanged. However, if an accidental is added to only one of the pitches, a different interval quality results. In each box, learn the intervals on the white keys of the keyboard before you study the sections on accidentals.

Of the intervals, 3rds, 6ths, 2nds, and 7ths are classified as *major* or *minor*; 4ths, 5ths, unisons, and octaves are classified as *perfect*. All *augmented* intervals are ½-step larger than major or perfect interval qualities. As shown in Example 6–3a, C to E is a major 3rd, but C to E♯ and C♭ to E are augmented 3rds, ½-step larger than major 3rds. *Diminished* intervals are ½-step smaller than minor or perfect intervals. In Example 6–3b, C to G is a perfect 5th, but C to G♭ and C♯ to G are diminished 5ths—½-step smaller.

EXAMPLE 6–3

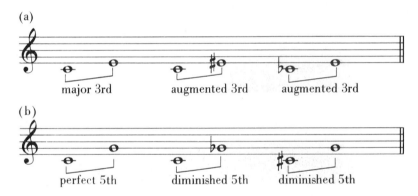

(a)

major 3rd   augmented 3rd   augmented 3rd

(b)

perfect 5th   diminished 5th   diminished 5th

All intervals have enharmonic equivalents. (*Note:* Remember from Chapter 2 that enharmonic tones sound the same but are spelled differently.) In Example 6–4, the augmented 2nd F to G♯ sounds the same as F

EXAMPLE 6–4

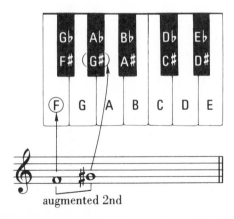

augmented 2nd

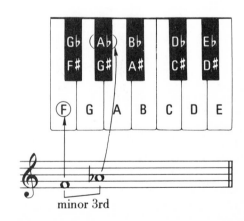

minor 3rd

to A♭, a minor 3rd. The spelling, however, is the determining factor. The intervals F to G and F to A are a 2nd and a 3rd, respectively, regardless of accidentals.

3rds Invert to 6ths

A *major 3rd* encompasses the distance of four half steps (Ex. 6-5*a*), while a *minor 6th* contains eight half steps (Ex. 6-5*b*).

EXAMPLE 6–5

(a)

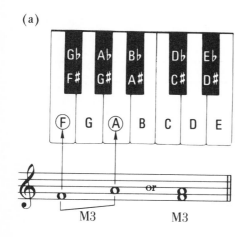

(b)

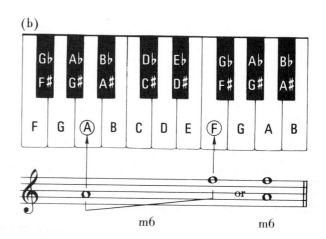

A *minor 3rd* encompasses the distance of three half steps (Ex. 6-6*a*), while a *major 6th* contains nine half steps (Ex. 6-6*b*).

EXAMPLE 6–6

(a)

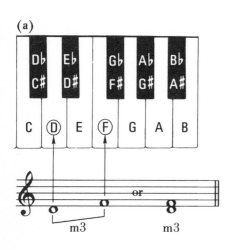

(b)

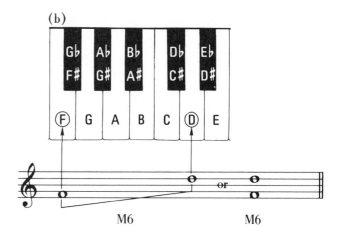

BOX 6–1

The following major 3rds and minor 6ths are possible on *white keys only* of the keyboard:

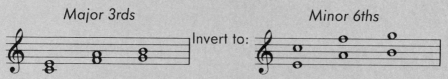

Adding like accidentals to *both* the top and the bottom tones does not change interval quality.

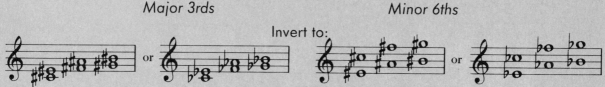

Lowering or raising *either* the top or the bottom tone changes interval quality.

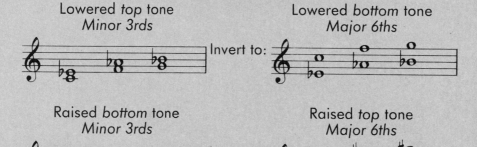

The following minor 3rds and major 6ths are possible on *white keys only* of the keyboard:

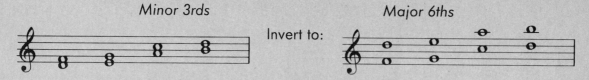

Adding like accidentals to *both* the top and the bottom tones does not change interval quality.

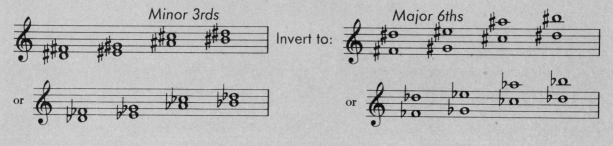

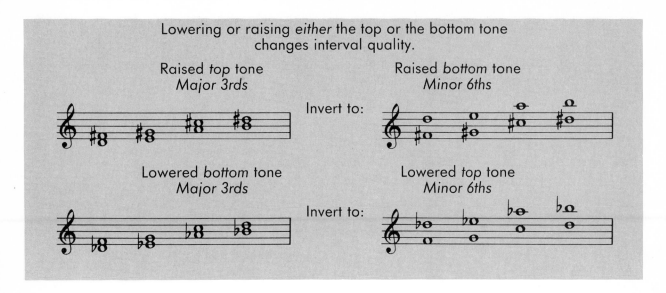

EXERCISE 6-1 As indicated, write either a major 3rd (M3), minor 6th (m6), minor 3rd (m3), or major 6th (M6) above each tone. Check answers in the left column.

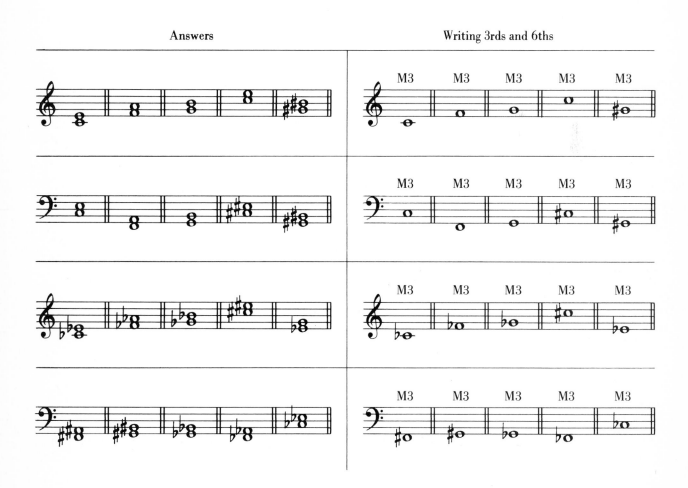

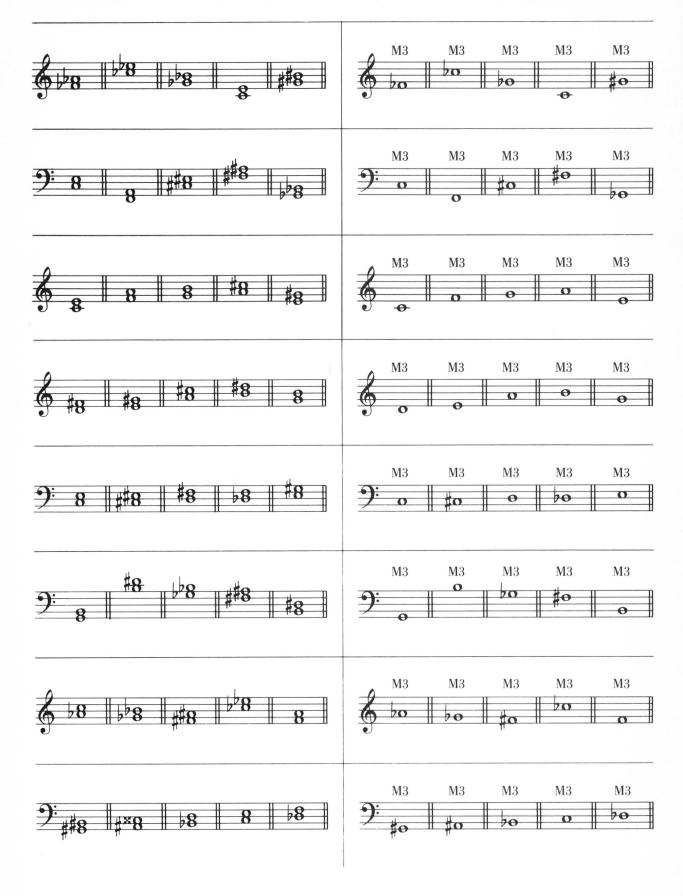

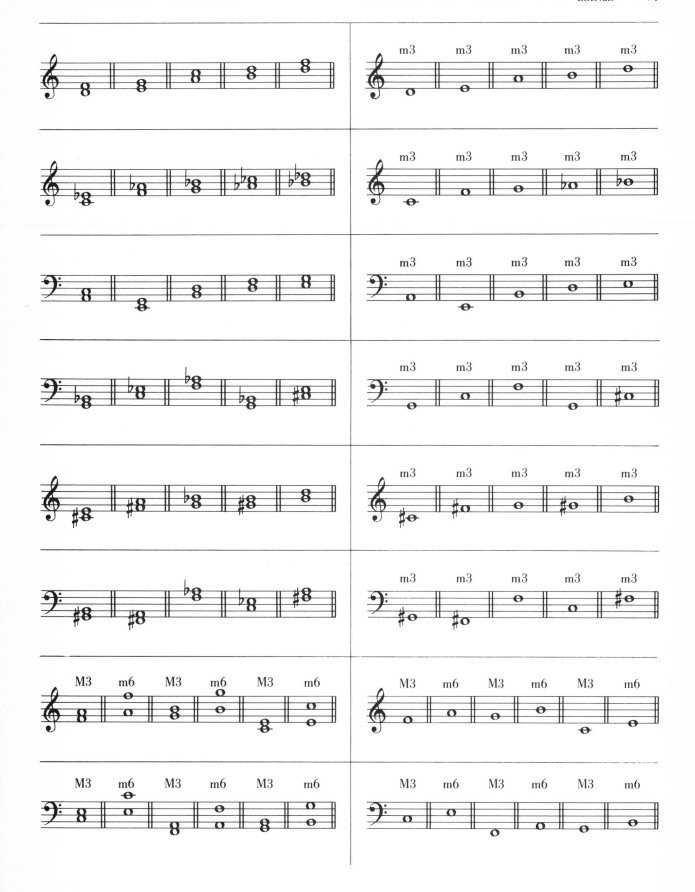

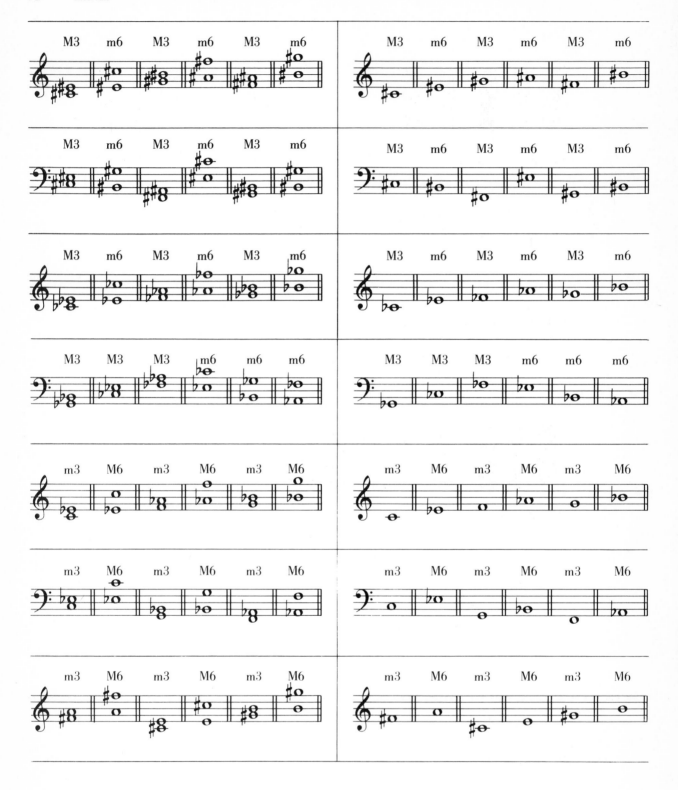

5ths Invert to 4ths

A *perfect 5th* encompasses the distance of seven half steps (Ex. 6-7*a*), while a *perfect 4th* contains five half steps (Ex. 6-7*b*).

EXAMPLE 6–7

(a)

(b)

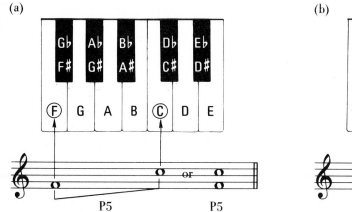
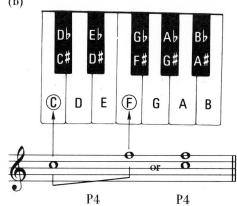

Depending on the spelling, the interval of six half steps is either a *diminished 5th* or an *augmented 4th*. As shown in Example 6–8, the distance from B up to F is the only diminished 5th possible on white keys; its inversion, F up to B, is the only augmented 4th possible on white keys. As will be seen in Box 6–3, all other diminished or augmented 5ths and 4ths require accidentals.

EXAMPLE 6–8

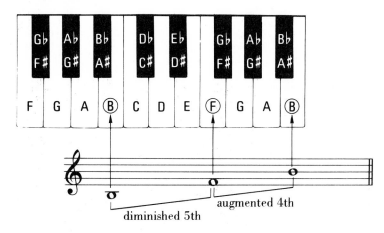

BOX 6–2

The following perfect 5ths and perfect 4ths are possible on *white keys only* of the keyboard:

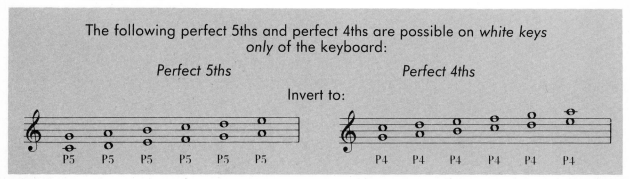

Adding like accidentals to *both* the top and the bottom tones does not change interval quality.

Perfect 5ths

Perfect 4ths

Invert to:

or

or

Lowering or raising *either* the top or the bottom tone changes interval quality.

Raised *top* tone
Augmented 5ths

Raised *bottom* tone
Diminished 4ths

Invert to:

Lowered *bottom* tone
Augmented 5ths

Lowered *top* tone
Diminished 4ths

Invert to:

Lowered *top* tone
Diminished 5ths

Lowered *bottom* tone
Augmented 4ths

Invert to:

Raised *bottom* tone
Diminished 5ths

Raised *top* tone
Augmented 4ths

Invert to:

The following diminished 5th and augmented 4th are possible on *white keys only* of the keyboard:

Diminished 5th

Augmented 4th

Inverts to:

Adding like accidentals to *both* the top and the bottom tones does not change interval quality.

Diminished 5th

Augmented 4th

Inverts to:

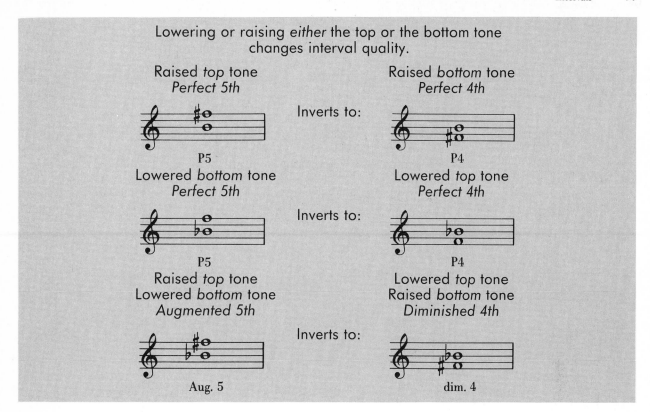

Lowering or raising *either* the top or the bottom tone changes interval quality.

◀EXERCISE 6-2 As indicated, write either a perfect 5th (P5), perfect 4th (P4), augmented 5th (A5), diminished 5th (d5), augmented 4th (A4), or diminished 4th (d4) above each tone in the right column. Check answers in the left column.

Answers   Writing 5ths and 4ths

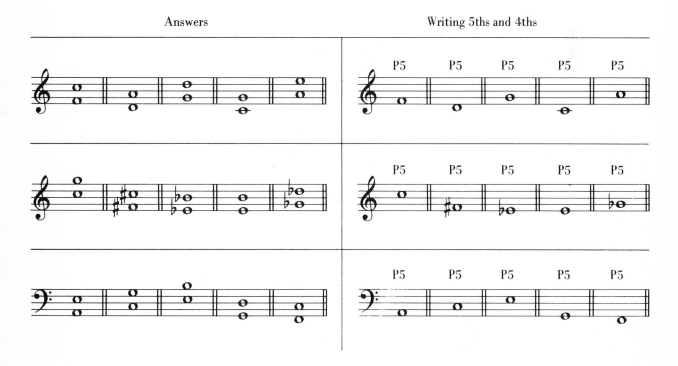

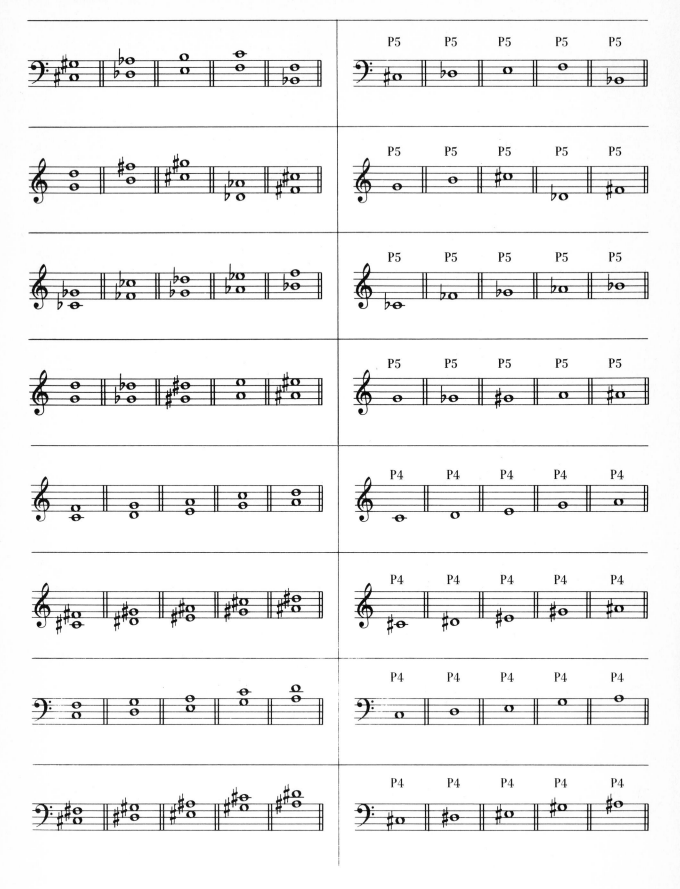

2nds Invert to 7ths

A *major 2nd* encompasses the distance of two half steps (Ex. 6-9*a*), while a *minor 7th* contains ten half steps (Ex. 6-9*b*).

EXAMPLE 6–9

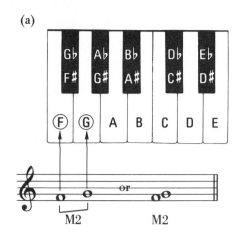

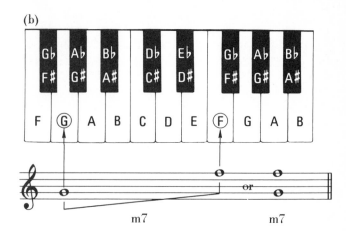

A minor 2nd encompasses the distance of one half step (Ex. 6-10*a*), while a major 7th contains eleven half steps (Ex. 6-10*b*).

EXAMPLE 6–10

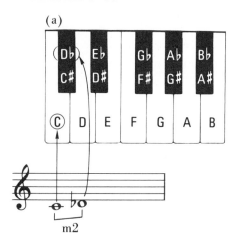

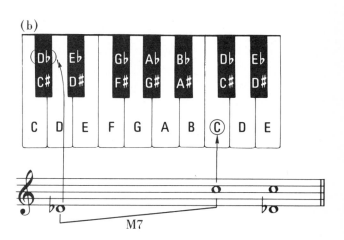

BOX 6–3

The following major 2nds and minor 7ths are possible on *white keys only* of the keyboard:

Major 2nds   *Minor 7ths*

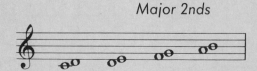   Invert to: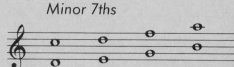

Adding like accidentals to *both* the top and the bottom tones does not change interval quality.

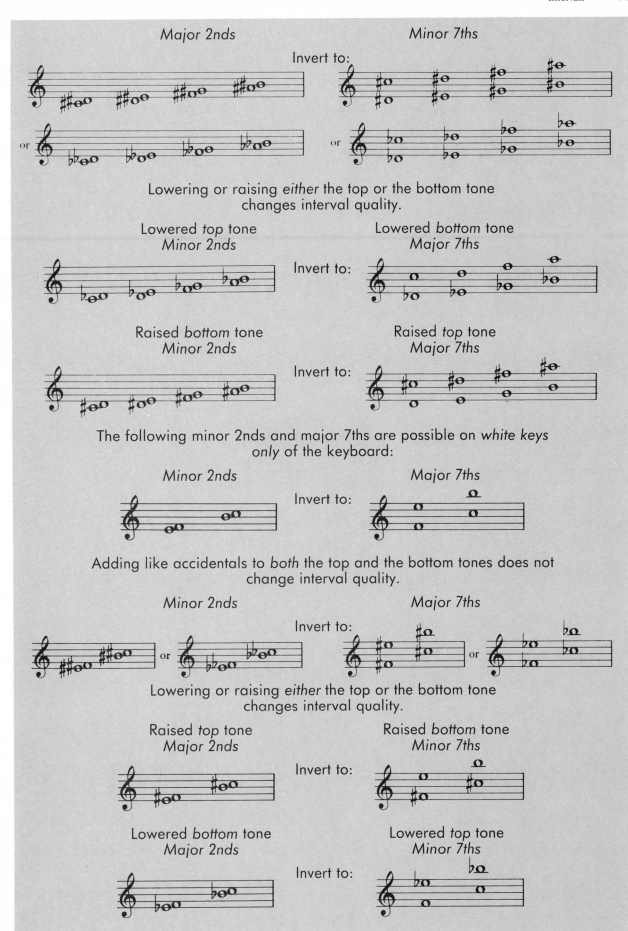

Major 2nds   Minor 7ths

Invert to:

or

Lowering or raising *either* the top or the bottom tone
changes interval quality.

Lowered *top* tone   Lowered *bottom* tone
Minor 2nds   Major 7ths

Invert to:

Raised *bottom* tone   Raised *top* tone
Minor 2nds   Major 7ths

Invert to:

The following minor 2nds and major 7ths are possible on *white keys
only* of the keyboard:

Minor 2nds   Major 7ths

Invert to:

Adding like accidentals to *both* the top and the bottom tones does not
change interval quality.

Minor 2nds   Major 7ths

Invert to: or

Lowering or raising *either* the top or the bottom tone
changes interval quality.

Raised *top* tone   Raised *bottom* tone
Major 2nds   Minor 7ths

Invert to:

Lowered *bottom* tone   Lowered *top* tone
Major 2nds   Minor 7ths

Invert to:

❰EXERCISE 6-3   As indicated, write either a major 2nd (M2), minor 7th (m7), minor 2nd (m2), or major 7th (M7) above each tone. Check answers in the left column.

Answers   Writing 2nds and 7ths

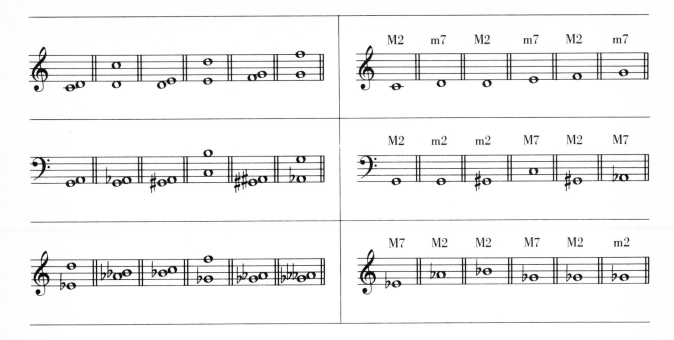

Unisons and Octaves

The unison (P1) and the octave (P8) are both perfect intervals. When two voices or instruments sound the same pitch, they are said to be in *unison* (Ex. 6-11*a*). The interval between any tone and the next tone with the same letter name is an *octave*—a distance of twelve half steps (Ex. 6-11*b*).

EXAMPLE 6–11

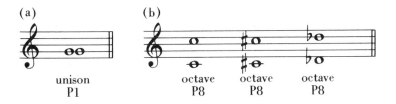

Compound Intervals

Intervals larger than an octave are called *compound intervals*. As shown in Example 6–12, intervals may be converted to compound intervals by adding an octave.

EXAMPLE 6–12

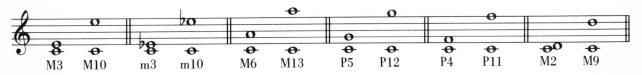

CHAPTER SEVEN
Introduction to Minor Scales

The minor scale, like the major, is identifiable by its unique pattern of whole and half steps. If you play from A to A on white keys only of the keyboard, you will notice that half steps lie between the 2nd and 3rd and the 5th and 6th scale degrees. The resultant *A-minor scale* (Ex. 7-1) is the only *natural* or *pure minor scale* that requires no sharps or flats.

EXAMPLE 7–1

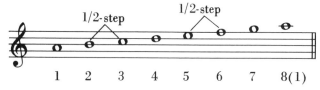

Remember from Chapter 3 that the only major scale possible on white keys of the keyboard is *C major*. In Example 7–2, the A minor scale is placed under the C-major scale to demonstrate how these two keys are related. The keys of C major and A minor are said to be *relative keys* because they share the same key signature (no sharps or flats). Therefore,

EXAMPLE 7–2

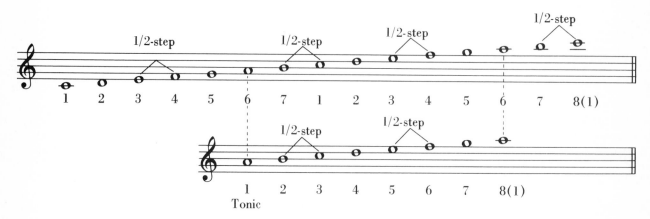

102

C major is the relative major of A minor, and A minor is the relative minor of C major. Because the tonic of the A-minor scale is the 6th degree of the C-major scale, the distance between the tonics of these relative keys is the interval of a minor 3rd (Ex. 7-3). (For a review of minor 3rds, refer to Box 6–1.) The relationship between C major and A minor applies to all other pairs of relative major and minor keys; each major key has a relative minor key that shares its key signature. To determine the key signature for any minor key, you must first find the tonic of its relative major, which is always a minor 3rd above the tonic of the minor key.

EXAMPLE 7–3

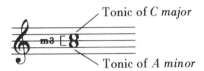

When the key signature with the appropriate sharps or flats is placed on the staff, the pattern of the natural minor scale (half steps between 2 and 3, and 5 and 6) is established automatically. For example, the relative major of the key of D minor is F major, with one flat (B♭) in its key signature. Writing from D to D on the staff with a key signature of one flat produces the *D natural minor scale* (Ex. 7-4).

EXAMPLE 7–4

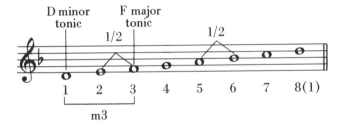

Relative Keys with Both Tonics on White Keys of the Keyboard

The relative keys to be studied in this section are those which have their *tonics* on *white keys only* of the keyboard. The tonics of these keys correspond to the minor 3rds possible on white keys of the keyboard (Ex. 7-5). The keys of A minor and C major, discussed in the previous section, belong in this set of four pairs of relative keys. The keys of D, E, and B minor, along with their relative majors, also have tonics on white keys of the keyboard. As seen in Example 7–6, when the key signatures are determined, the scales may be written accordingly.

EXAMPLE 7–5

(a) Relative keys with tonics on white keys only of the keyboard

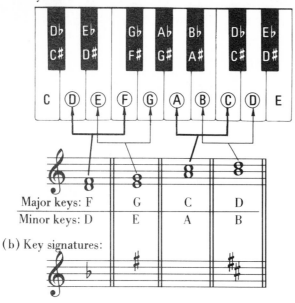

(b) Key signatures:

EXAMPLE 7–6

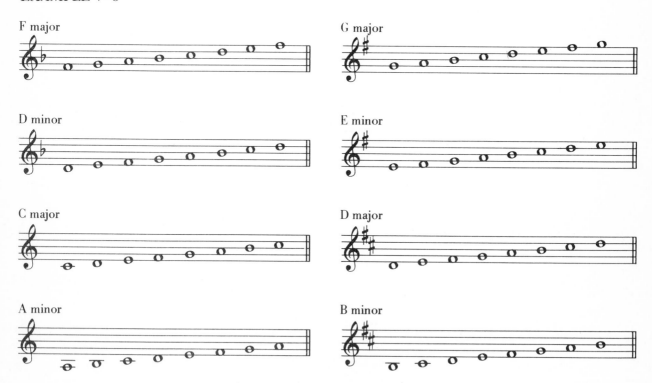

F major

G major

D minor

E minor

C major

D major

A minor

B minor

◖**EXERCISE 7-1**   After studying the pairs of scales in Example 7–6, write the following minor scales in the space provided in the right column. Before writing each scale, determine the proper key signature and place it on the staff. Check scales with answers in the left column.

Answers	Writing minor scales

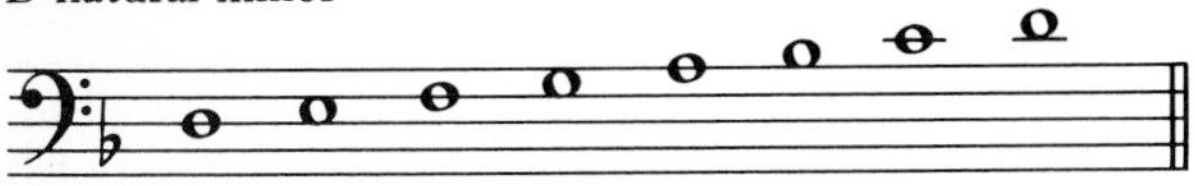

D natural minor

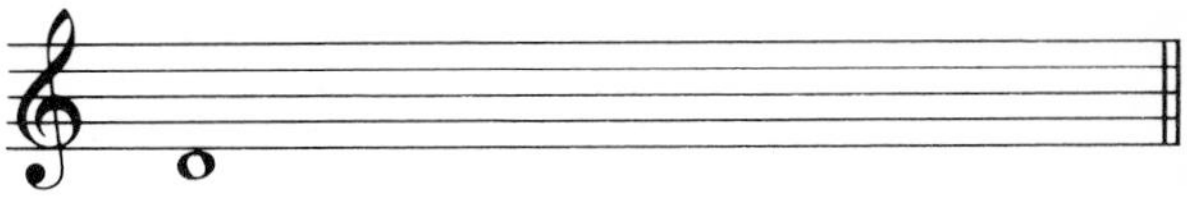

D natural minor

A natural minor

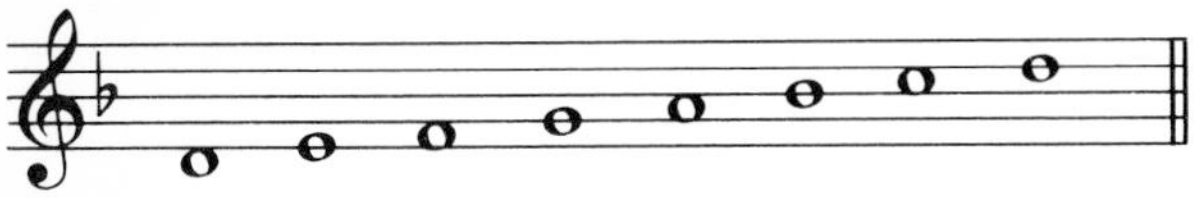

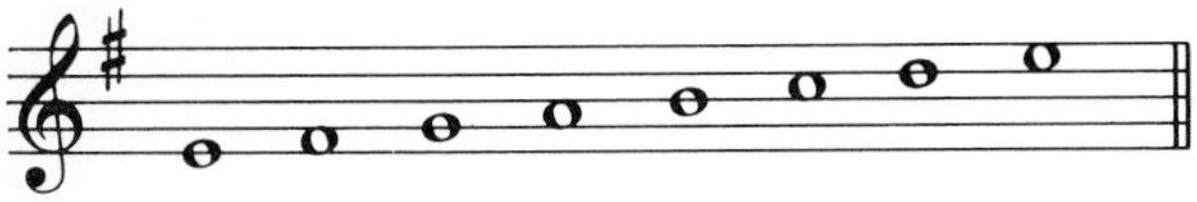

A natural minor

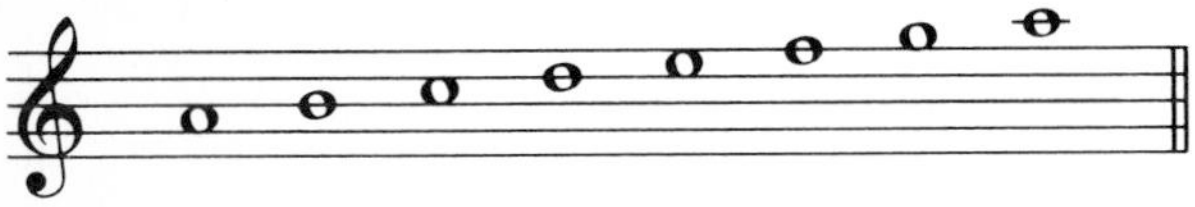

B natural minor

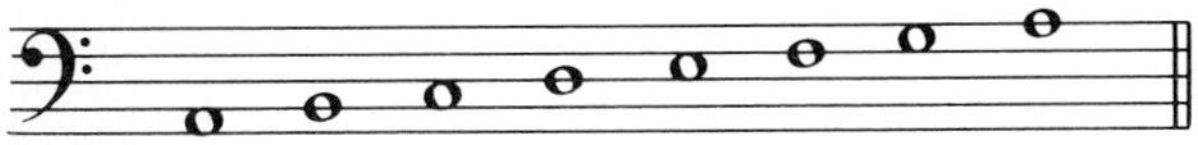

B natural minor

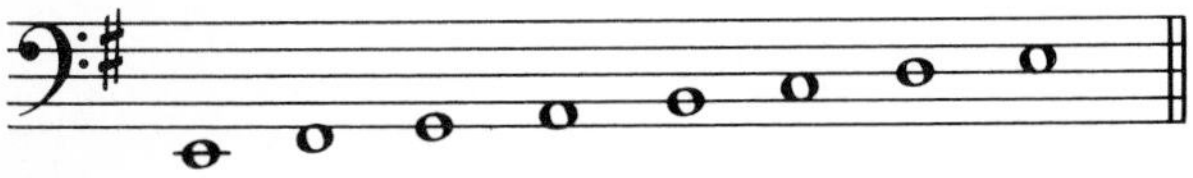

E natural minor

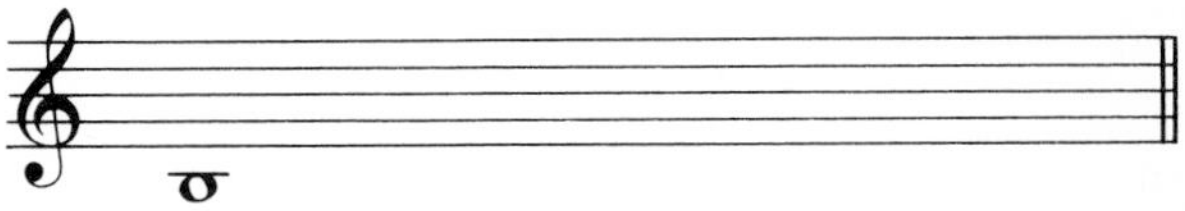

E natural minor

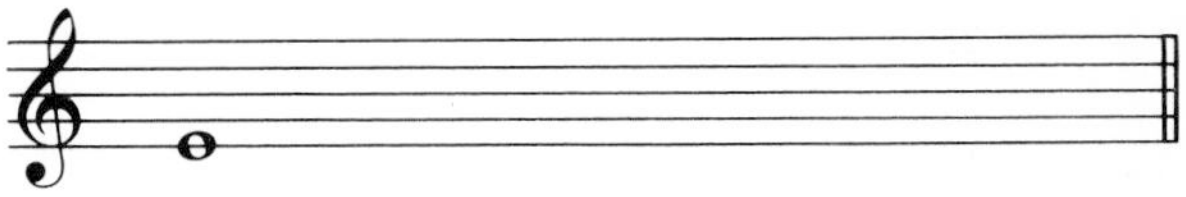

A natural minor

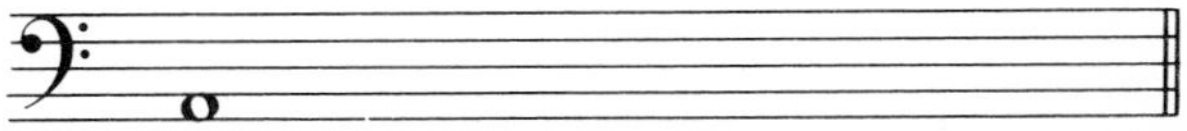

A natural minor

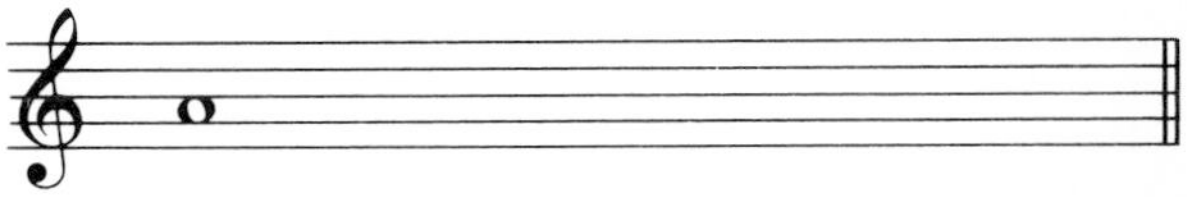

B natural minor

B natural minor

E natural minor

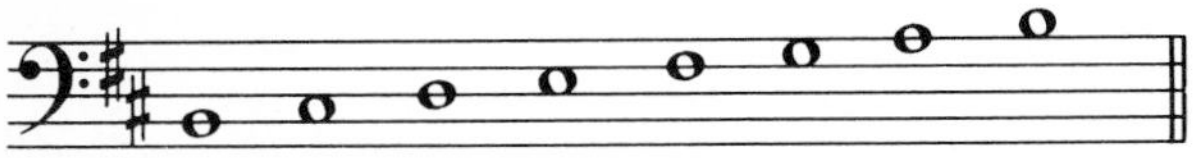

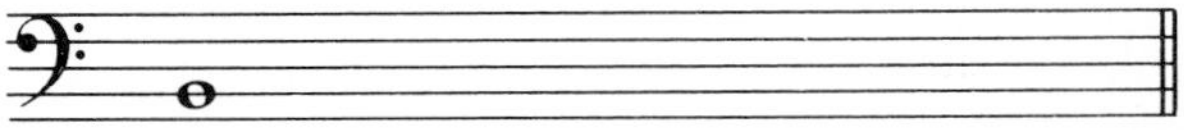

E natural minor

D natural minor

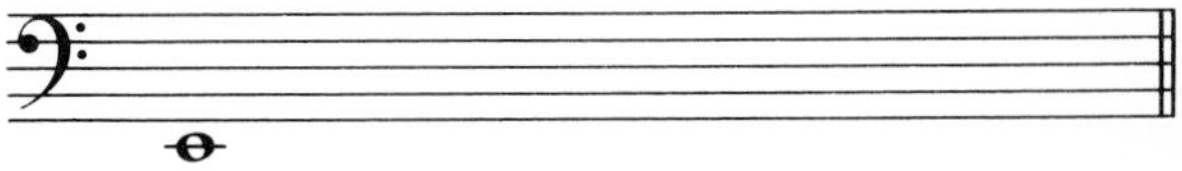

D natural minor

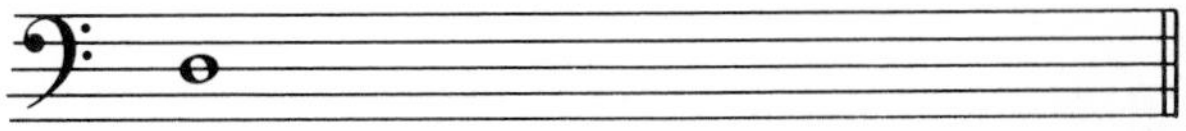

Other Forms of the Minor Scale

Two additional forms of the minor scale are the *melodic minor* and the *harmonic minor*. The melodic minor scale is the same basic scale as the natural or pure minor, but with the *6th and 7th scale degrees* raised when the melody ascends. This alteration is made in order to supply a half step between the 7th degree (leading tone) and the tonic. The 6th and 7th degrees are restored to their regular positions when the melody descends (Ex. 7-7).

EXAMPLE 7–7

(a) *Pure* or *natural minor*

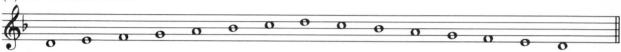

(b) *Melodic minor*

(c) *Harmonic minor*

The harmonic minor scale is also similar to the natural minor scale, with the exception that the *7th degree only* is raised—both ascending and descending. Note that all three forms of the minor scale have identical key signatures.

❨**EXERCISE 7-2** In the right column, the D, E, A, and B *natural* minor scales are provided. Below each natural minor scale, write the *melodic* and *harmonic* minor scale forms, ascending and descending. Check answers in the left column.

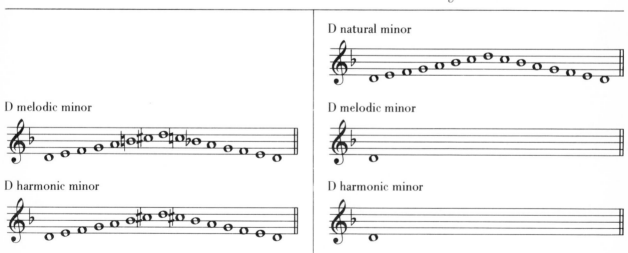

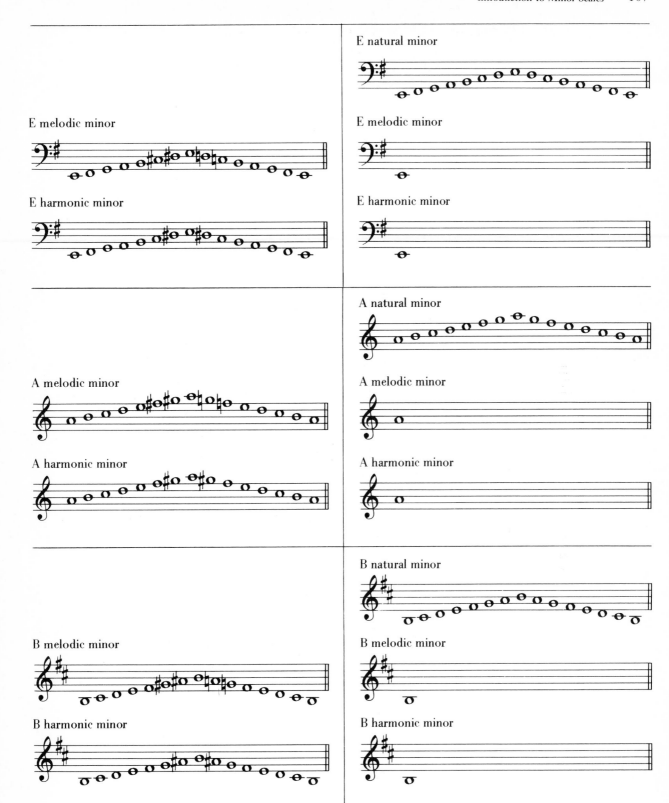

◖EXERCISE 7-3 The following melodies are limited to the keys of D, E, A, and B minor and include all three minor scale forms—natural, melodic, and harmonic. If necessary, review rhythm and meter in Chapter 1.

Suggested study:

1. Determine the minor key and its scale form (natural, melodic, or harmonic).
2. Circle triad tones (1, 3, 5) and label embellishing tones (PT, UN, LN).
3. Sing the triad tones.
4. Observing the meter, clap the rhythm.
5. Sing the melody.

O COME, O COME, EMMANUEL

Gregorian melody

O come, O come, Em - man - u - el,   And ran - som cap - tive Is - ra - el,

Options for Further Study

Two options are suggested at this point, depending upon individual needs or course objectives. If desired, turn to Chapter 8, "Harmonizing Simple Melodies," and begin the study of harmonization using only the most common major and minor keys covered thus far. Or, continue with this chapter and study the remaining minor keys.

The Remaining Minor Keys

As discussed in the previous section, minor keys with tonics on D, E, A, and B have relative major keys with tonics one minor 3rd higher on F, G, C, and D, respectively (Ex. 7-8*a*). This minor-3rd relationship between the tonics of relative keys is retained if both tonics are flatted or both are sharped. Theoretically, then, minor keys with tonics on D♭, E♭, A♭, and B♭ have relative majors with tonics on F♭, G♭, C♭, and D♭ (Ex. 7-8*b*). Likewise, as summarized in Example 7–8*c*, minor keys with tonics on D♯, E♯, A♯, and B♯ have relative majors with tonics on F♯, G♯, C♯, and D♯. Remember from Chapter 3, however, that keys with more than seven sharps or flats are impractical because each has an *enharmonic* key with fewer sharps or flats. For example, F-flat major, with eight flats, is *enharmonically equivalent* (sounds the same, but is spelled differently) to E major, with only four sharps.

EXAMPLE 7–8

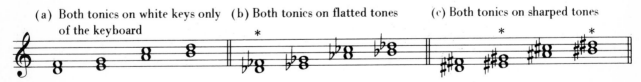

(a) Both tonics on white keys only of the keyboard   (b) Both tonics on flatted tones   (c) Both tonics on sharped tones

* Impractical keys

Relative Keys with Both Tonics on Flatted Tones

Both tonics of relative major and minor keys may be on flatted tones. Learn the key signatures in Example 7–9 before studying the corresponding pairs of scales in Example 7–10. Although only the *natural* form of each minor scale is given, the *melodic* and *harmonic* forms may be written by adding the appropriate accidentals. (If necessary, review the earlier section "Other Forms of the Minor Scale," on p. 105.)

EXAMPLE 7–9

(a) Relative keys with tonics on flatted tones

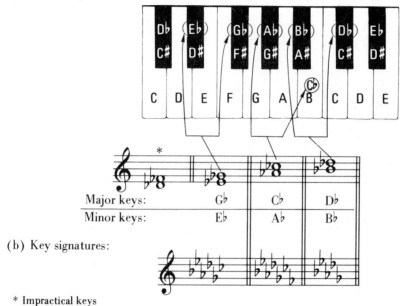

Major keys:	Gb	Cb	Db
Minor keys:	Eb	Ab	Bb

(b) Key signatures:

* Impractical keys

EXAMPLE 7–10

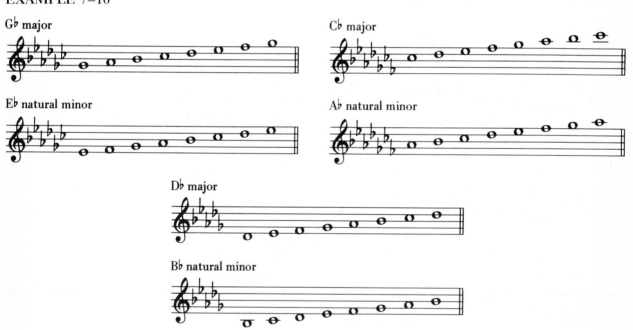

Gb major

Cb major

Eb natural minor

Ab natural minor

Db major

Bb natural minor

❬EXERCISE 7-4   After studying the pairs of scales in Example 7–10, practice writing the following minor scales in the space provided in the right column. Before writing each scale, determine the proper key signature and write it on the staff. Check written scales with answers in the left column.

Answers	Writing minor scales

E♭ melodic minor

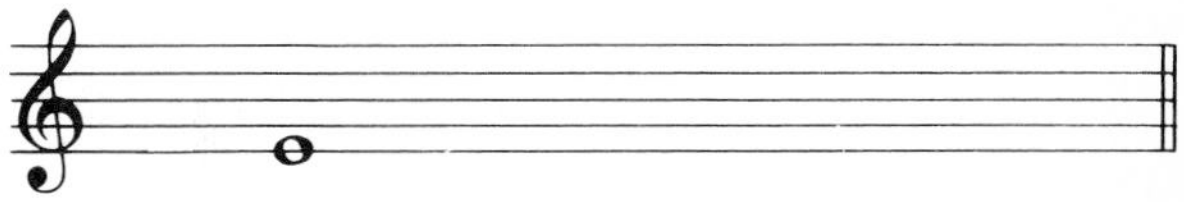

E♭ melodic minor

A♭ harmonic minor

A♭ harmonic minor

B♭ natural minor

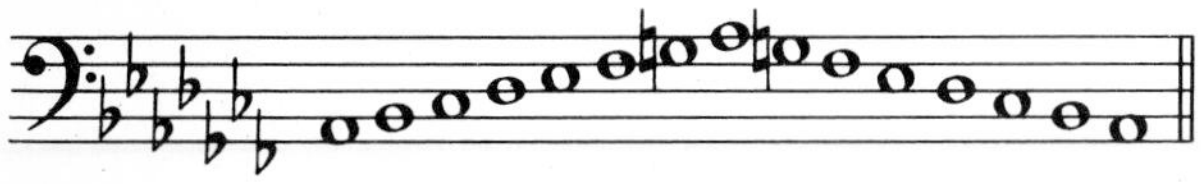

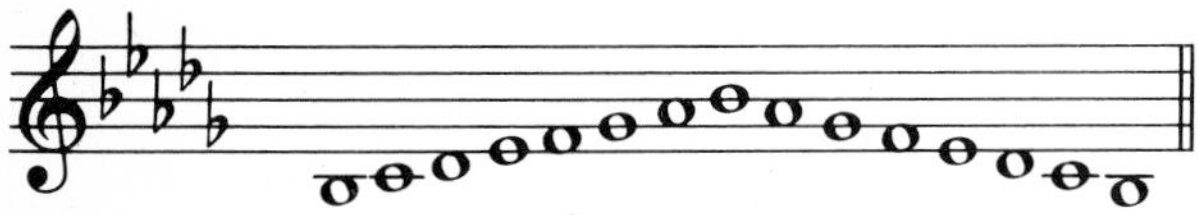

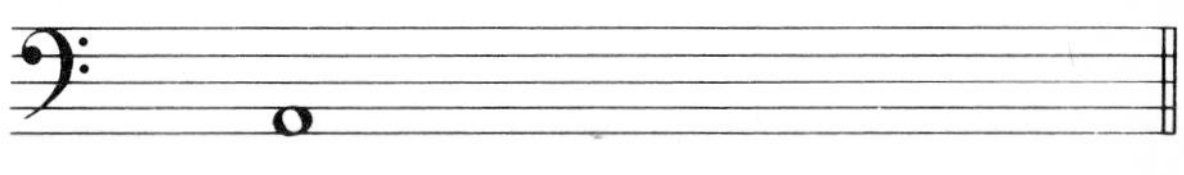

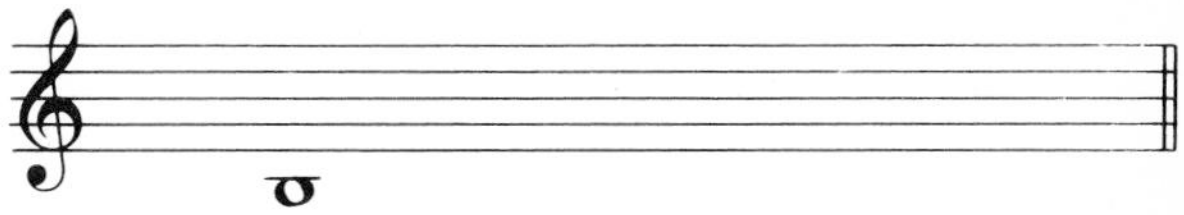

B♭ natural minor

B♭ melodic minor

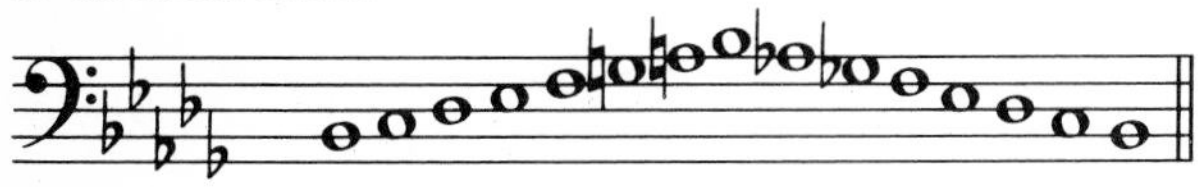

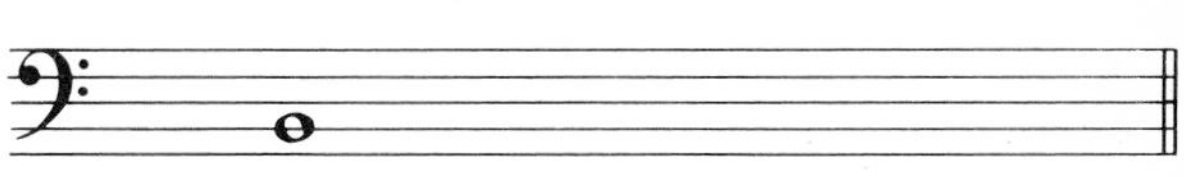

B♭ melodic minor

E♭ melodic minor

E♭ melodic minor

E♭ natural minor

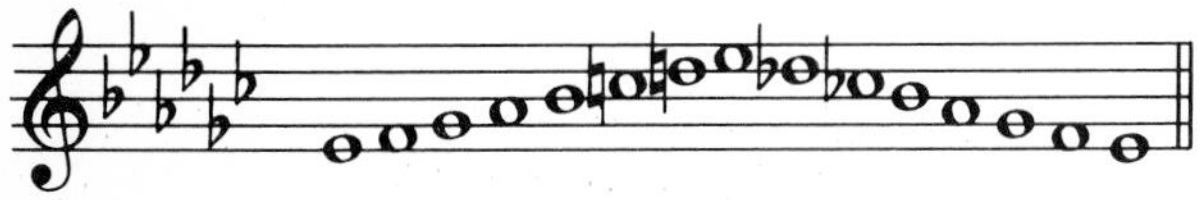

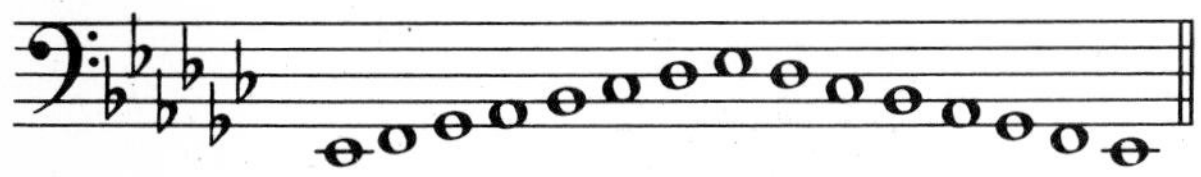

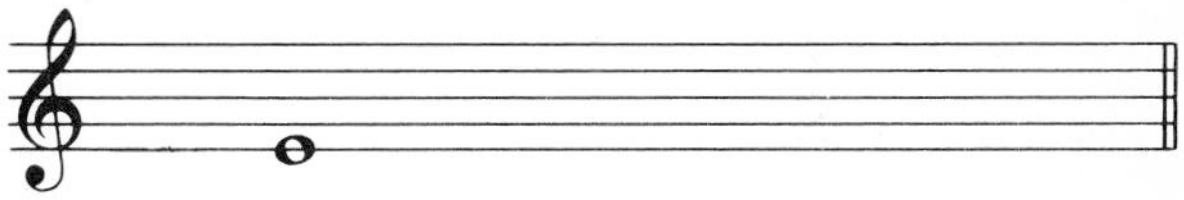

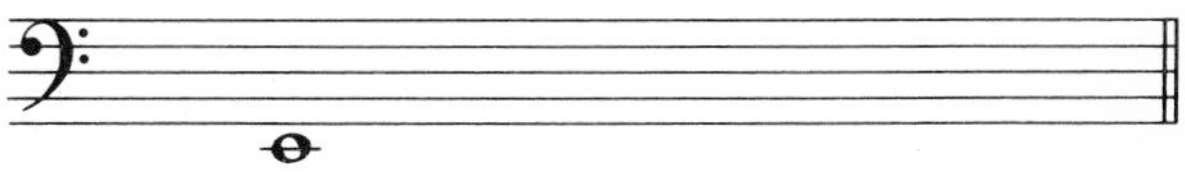

E♭ natural minor

A♭ harmonic minor

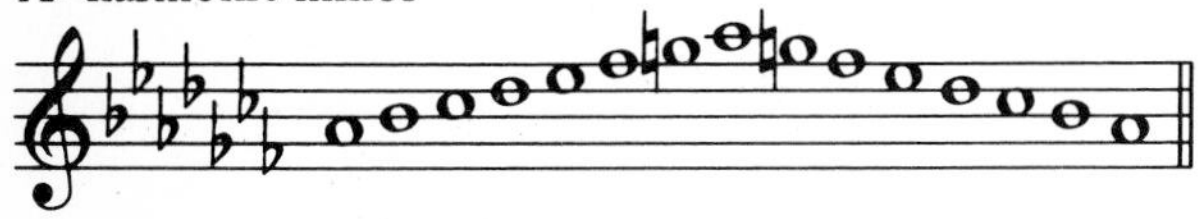

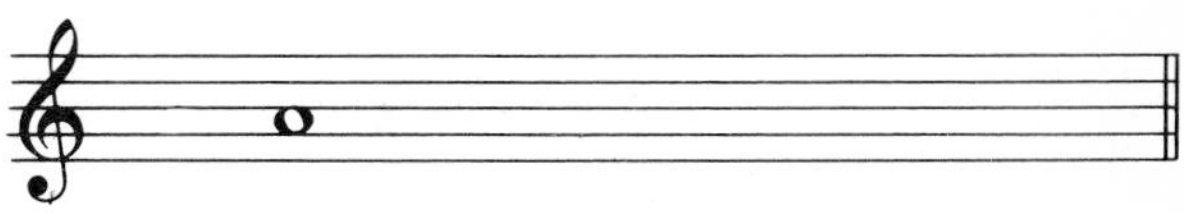

A♭ harmonic minor

E♭ harmonic minor

E♭ harmonic minor

B♭ natural minor

B♭ natural minor

A♭ melodic minor

A♭ melodic minor

Relative Keys with Both Tonics on Sharped Tones

Both tonics of relative major and minor keys may also be on sharped tones. Learn the key signatures in Example 7–11 before studying the corresponding scales in Example 7–12. Only the natural form of each minor scale is given; for the melodic and harmonic forms the appropriate accidentals must be added.

EXAMPLE 7–11

(a) Relative keys with both tonics on a sharped tone

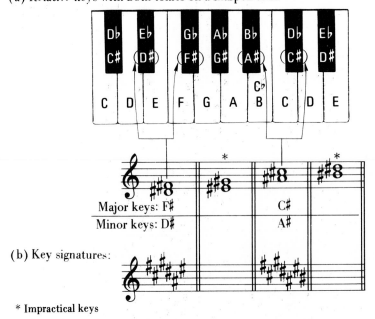

Major keys: F♯   C♯

Minor keys: D♯   A♯

(b) Key signatures:

* Impractical keys

EXAMPLE 7–12

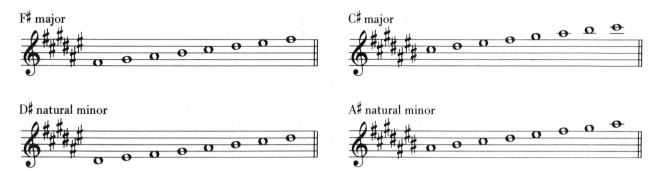

F♯ major

C♯ major

D♯ natural minor

A♯ natural minor

◖EXERCISE 7-5 After studying the pairs of scales in Example 7–12, practice writing the following minor scales in the right column. Before writing each scale, determine the proper key signature and place it on the staff. Check written scales with answers in the left column.

Answers	Writing minor scales
A♯ harmonic minor	A♯ harmonic minor
D♯ melodic minor	D♯ melodic minor
A♯ natural minor	A♯ natural minor
D♯ melodic minor	D♯ melodic minor
D♯ harmonic minor	D♯ harmonic minor

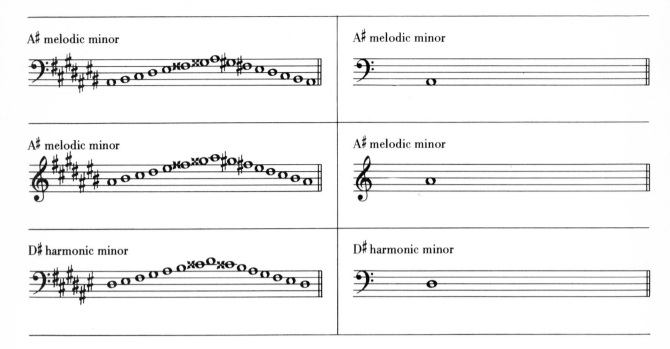

A♯ melodic minor

A♯ melodic minor

A♯ melodic minor

A♯ melodic minor

D♯ harmonic minor

D♯ harmonic minor

Thus far, all relative major and minor keys have been studied in relation to the minor 3rds possible on white keys only of the keyboard—minor 3rds built on D, E, A, and B. Using these same four letter names, the minor 3rd relationship is retained if both tonics are flatted or both are sharped. Hence, minor keys with tonics on D♭, E♭, A♭, B♭, D♯, E♯, A♯, and B♯ have relative majors with tonics on F♭, G♭, C♭, D♭, F♯, G♯, C♯ and D♯, respectively. However, as seen in Examples 7–8, 7–9, and 7–11, some of these keys are impractical.

Relative Keys with Only One Tonic on a White Key of the Keyboard

As shown in Example 7–13, the remaining 3rds on the white keys only of the keyboard are *major 3rds*—3rds built on C, F, and G. (For a review of major 3rds, refer to Box 6–1.) Because the tonics of relative major and minor keys are a *minor 3rd* apart, minor keys with tonics on C, F, or G must have relative majors with tonics on E♭, A♭, or B♭, respectively. Only the tonics of the minor keys in each of these pairs are on white keys of the

EXAMPLE 7–13

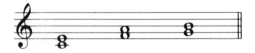

keyboard. As shown in Example 7–14, to preserve the minor 3rd relationship between tonics, the tonic of the relative major must be a flatted tone. Learn the key signatures in Example 7–14 before studying the three pairs of scales in Example 7–15. Although not given in the example, the melodic and harmonic forms are also possible for each of these minor scales.

EXAMPLE 7–14

(a) Relative keys with tonics of majors on flatted tones

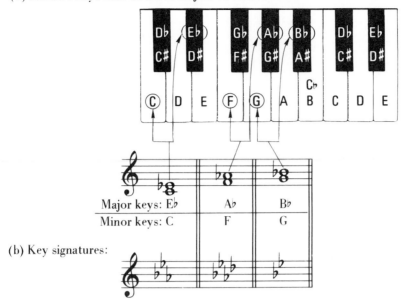

(b) Key signatures:

EXAMPLE 7–15

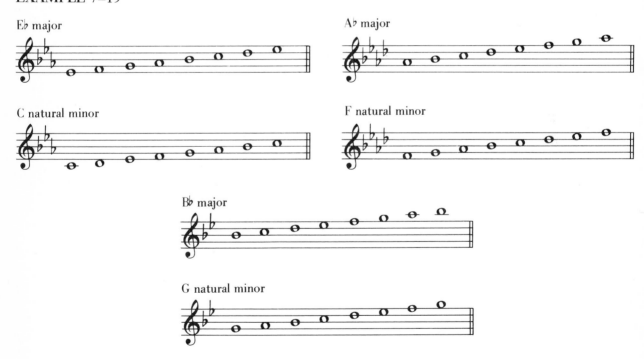

EXERCISE 7-6   After studying the pairs of scales in Example 7–15, write the following minor scales in the right column. Before writing each scale, determine the proper key signature and place it on the staff. Check written scales with answers in the left column.

116   *Introduction to Minor Scales*

Answers   Writing minor scales

C natural minor   C natural minor

F melodic minor   F melodic minor

G harmonic minor   G harmonic minor

G melodic minor   G melodic minor

C melodic minor   C melodic minor

C harmonic minor   C harmonic minor

F natural minor   F natural minor

G natural minor   G natural minor

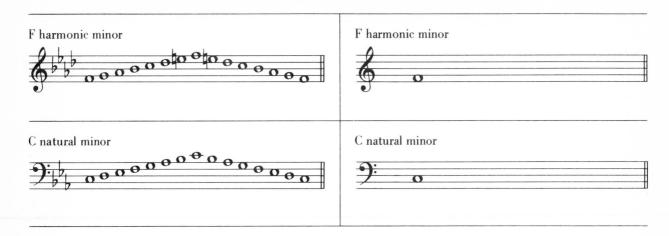

F harmonic minor

C natural minor

F harmonic minor

C natural minor

As shown in Example 7–16, the three remaining major keys with tonics on white keys of the keyboard (E, A, and B) have relative minor keys with tonics on sharped tones (C♯, F♯, and G♯). Learn the key signatures in Example 7–16 before studying the pairs of scales in Example 7–17.

EXAMPLE 7–16

(a) Relative keys with tonics of minors on sharped tones

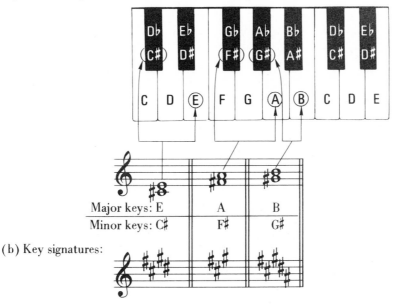

| Major keys: | E | A | B |
| Minor keys: | C♯ | F♯ | G♯ |

(b) Key signatures:

EXAMPLE 7–17

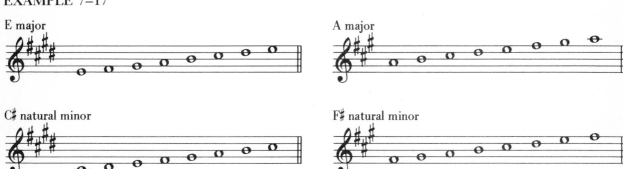

E major

C♯ natural minor

A major

F♯ natural minor

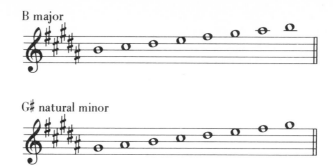

B major

G# natural minor

◖EXERCISE 7-7   After studying the pairs of scales in Example 7–17, write the following minor scales in the right column. Before writing each scale, determine the proper key signature and place it on the staff. Check written scales with answers in the left column.

Answers	Writing minor scales
F# harmonic minor	F# harmonic minor
C# melodic minor	C# melodic minor
F# natural minor	F# natural minor
G# natural minor	G# natural minor
C# harmonic minor	C# harmonic minor

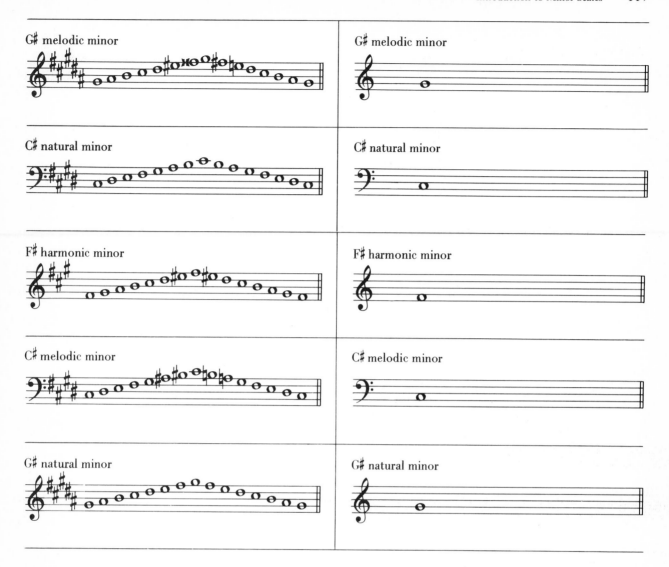

Parallel Major and Minor Keys

A minor scale and its *relative* major, as discussed in the previous sections, share a common key signature but have different tonics. A minor scale and its *parallel* major, on the other hand, share common tonics but have different key signatures. As shown in Example 7–18, the relative major of C minor is E-flat major; the parallel major of C minor is C major. Likewise, the parallel minor of any major key shares a common tonic and thus the same key name. Compare the parallel major and minor scales in Example 7–19. For a review of the procedure for determining key signatures for minor keys, refer to the discussion at the beginning of this chapter.

In musical compositions, changes between parallel keys provide the contrast of major and minor qualities without destroying the basic tonality. A well-known example of this contrast in parallel keys is found in "I Love Paris," Example 7–20. The first sixteen measures are in the key of C minor. In measure 17, notice the key change to C major.

EXAMPLE 7–18

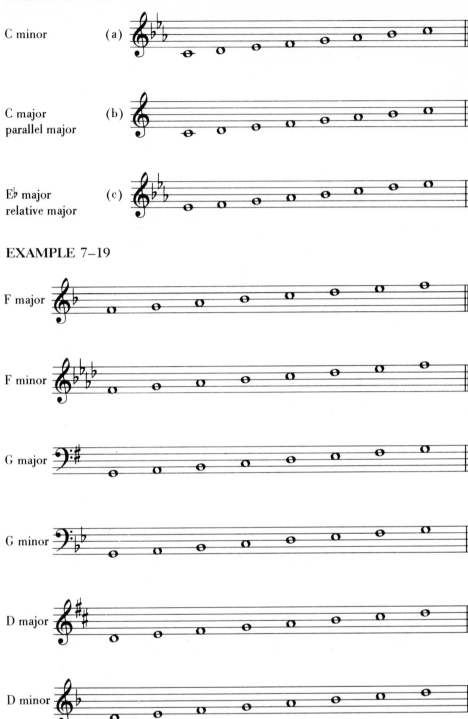

C minor   (a)

C major   (b)
parallel major

E♭ major   (c)
relative major

EXAMPLE 7–19

F major

F minor

G major

G minor

D major

D minor

Another famous example occurs in Haydn's Symphony No. 94 (*Surprise*). The second movement is a theme with a set of variations. The theme, Example 7–21*a*, is stated at the beginning of the movement. In the second variation, Example 7–21*b*, the key changes from C major to its parallel minor, C minor.

EXAMPLE 7–20

I LOVE PARIS

Words and music by Cole Porter

EXAMPLE 7–21

Blues Scale

One of the most apparent mixtures of parallel major and minor scales occurs in jazz and popular music based on the *blues scale*. Because the

EXAMPLE 7–22

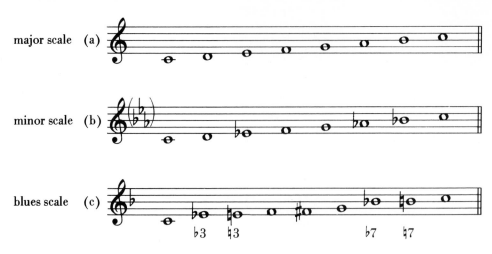

most common form of the scale contains both the minor and major versions of the 3rd and 7th degrees, it seems to be a mixture of the parallel major and minor scales (Ex. 7-22*a*, *b*, and *c*).

❰EXERCISE 7-8   Convert each of the following major scales into its parallel minor scale. Check answers in the left column.

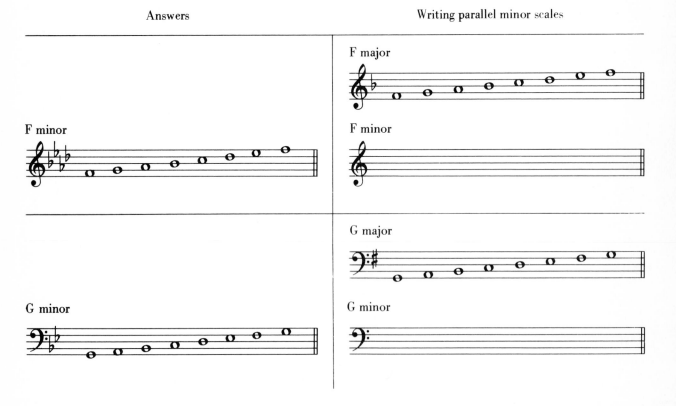

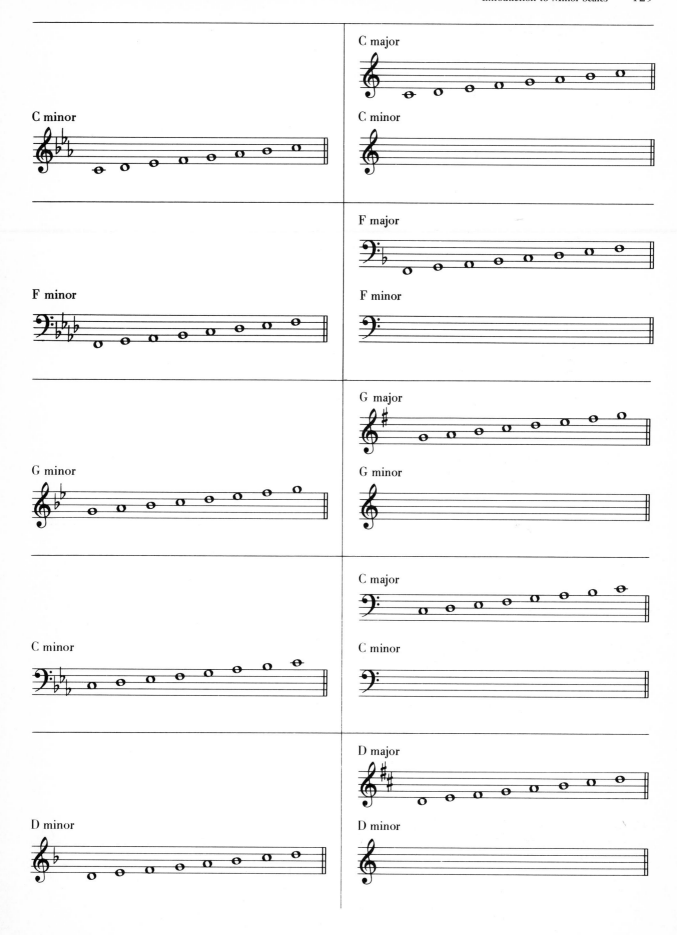

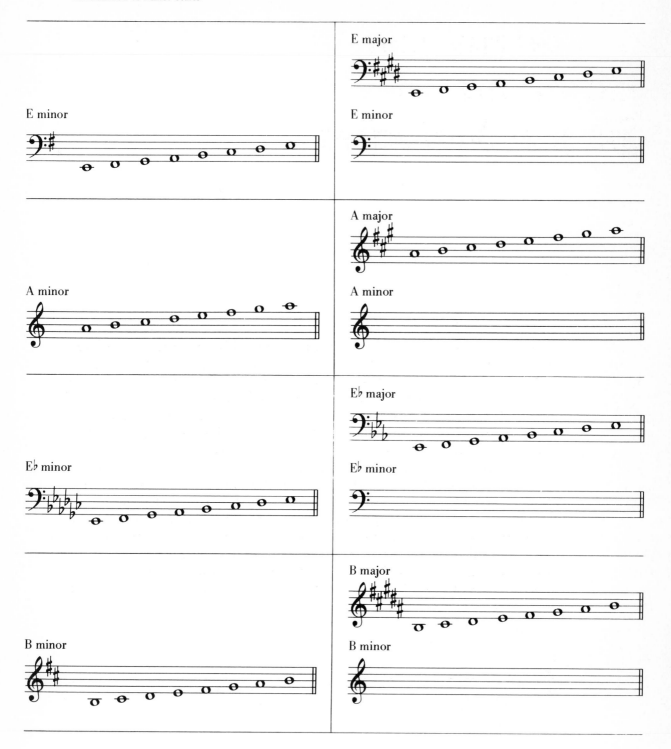

CHAPTER EIGHT
Harmonizing Simple Melodies

Few melodies are meant to stand alone without some sort of background, or accompaniment. For example, a folk singer may be accompanied by a guitarist or other instrumentalist; a violinist may be accompanied by a pianist. Even a large orchestra has at times a principal melody for solo instrument accompanied by the other instruments.

Accompaniment material usually consists of harmonies that have tones in common with the melodic line. Many of the melodies in previous chapters were based on horizontal outlines of triads, or *chords*, especially the chord built on the tonic of the melody. Because it is built on the 1st scale degree, the tonic triad is designated by the uppercase roman numeral "I" in major keys and the lowercase roman numeral "i" in minor keys (Ex. 8-1*a* and *b*). (Likewise, two other commonly used chords, the IV and V, are so called because they are built on the 4th and 5th scale degrees, respectively. In this chapter, however, melodies will outline the tonic triad only. Harmonizing with the IV and V triads is reserved for Chapter 9.)

EXAMPLE 8–1

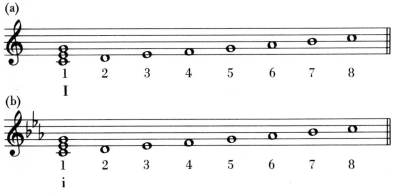

If the harmonic form of the tonic triad is sounded along with the melodic form, as in Example 8–2*a* and *b*, the melody is said to be

125

EXAMPLE 8–2

(a)

C major

(b)

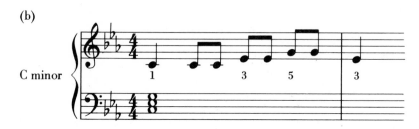

C minor

harmonized. Knowledge of harmonization techniques is essential for the composer or arranger, or for anyone who is interested in learning how to construct accompaniments.

Melodies in Three Common Major Keys

Before harmonizing a melody, you must determine which triad tones it contains. In Example 8–3*a*, the 1st, 3rd, and 5th scale degrees of the G-major triad are outlined horizontally, or melodically. Each of these melody tones is harmonized without rhythm in Example 8–3*b* by placing the two remaining triad tones beneath.

EXAMPLE 8–3

(a)   (b)

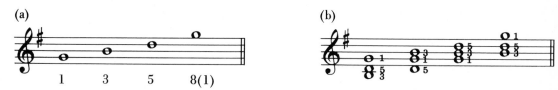

In Example 8–4, the 1st, 3rd, and 5th scale degrees are harmonized using the tonic triad; the remaining scale tones are treated as passing tones. The same considerations for harmonizing scale degrees apply to all other keys. The introduction of the IV and V triads in Chapter 9 will present many new possibilities for harmonizing all tones of the scale.

EXAMPLE 8–4

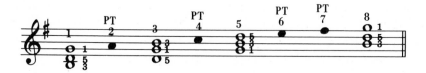

Melodies with Embellishing Tones

Example 8–5, in G major, contains melodic fragments harmonized with the tonic triad. The fragments are based on tones of the tonic triad, but also include passing tones and neighbor tones. In *a* and *b*, the 5th scale degree is harmonized. Staff *c* features harmonization of the 3rd scale degree, while lines *d*, *e*, and *f* have a mixture of the 1st, 3rd, and 5th scale degrees harmonized.

EXAMPLE 8–5

⟪EXERCISE 8-1   Before harmonizing each of the following melodies, determine the key (all are in major keys). Label all tones of the tonic triad (1–3–5) and all passing tones (PT) and neighbor tones (UN, LN). Using Example 8–5 as a model, harmonize each melody.

Melodies in Three Common Minor Keys

The principles outlined for harmonizing melodies in major keys also apply to harmonizing melodies in minor keys. Recall that each key signature indicates either a major key or its relative minor key. Although the key signature of one flat in Example 8–6 could indicate the key of F major, the triad outline and harmonization of the notes D, F, and A

EXAMPLE 8–6

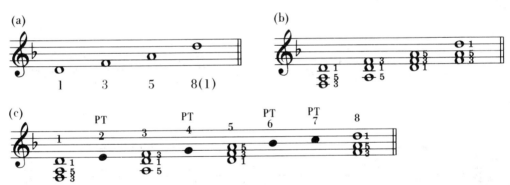

establish D minor as the key. The key signature of one sharp in Example 8–7 could indicate the key of G major. As shown in the analysis on the lower staff, however, the melody outlines the E minor triad and ends on the note E. The melody in Example 8–7, then, is in the key of E minor and is harmonized with the tonic triad, E–G–B. Remember that the 7th scale degree is often raised in minor keys. (If necessary, refer to "Other Forms of the Minor Scale" in Chapter 7.)

EXAMPLE 8–7

⟨EXERCISE 8-2   Using Examples 8–6 and 8–7 as a guide, harmonize the following melodies in minor keys. Label all tones of the tonic triad (1–3–5) and all passing tones (PT) and neighbor tones (UN, LN).

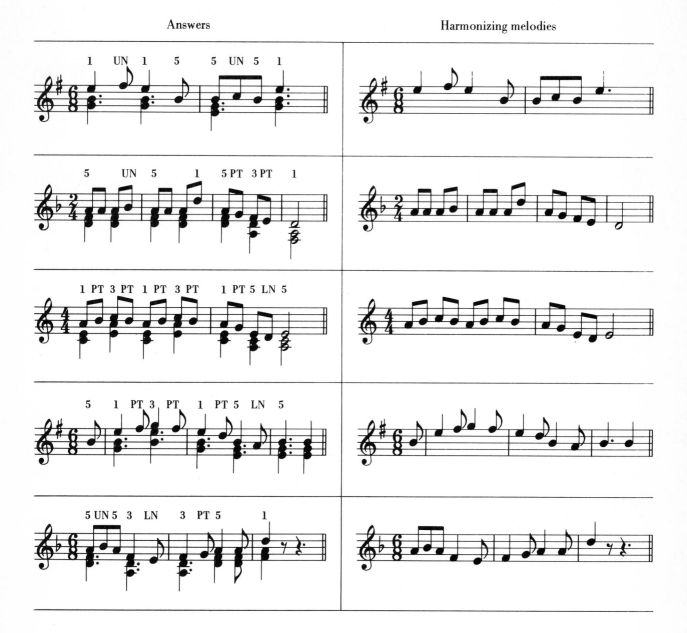

Answers   Harmonizing melodies

Options for Further Study

At this point you have two options. You may proceed to Chapter 9 and study harmonizing melodies in common major and minor keys, with the I, IV, V, and V7 chords, or you may continue with this chapter and harmonize melodies with the tonic triad in additional keys.

❰EXERCISE 8-3   Using the tonic triad only, harmonize the following major and minor melodies. For a review of the procedure for determining whether a melody is in a major or minor key, refer to Examples 8–6 and 8–7, and their explanations under "Harmonizing Melodies in Three Common Minor Keys." Label all passing tones and neighbor tones. Suggested solutions are given in the left column.

Answers   Harmonizing melodies

CHAPTER NINE
Harmonizing with the I, IV, V, and V⁷ Chords

In the previous chapter, the 1st, 3rd, and 5th scale degrees in melodies were harmonized with the tonic triad. The 2nd, 4th, 6th, and 7th degrees were treated as embellishing tones, meant only to enhance or enliven the simple melodies. Most melodic harmonizations, however, are not restricted to the tonic triad and are, therefore, much richer.

The triads built on the 4th and 5th scale degrees, the IV and V triads, respectively, are commonly used along with the I triad to harmonize melodies. Because the I, IV, and V triads (i, iv, and v or V in minor) collectively contain all tones of the scale (Ex. 9-1*a* and *b*), any scale degree may be harmonized by at least one of these three triads.

EXAMPLE 9–1

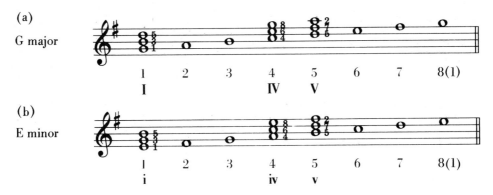

(a)
G major

(b)
E minor

Criteria for Choosing Harmonies

All discussion of the criteria for choosing harmonies will involve major keys only. Melodies in minor keys will be included for harmonization in the final section of this chapter.

Scale Degree

Example 9–2*a* summarizes the I, IV, and V chord choices according to scale degree in the melody. Notice in Example 9–2*b* that the I and IV triads have the 1st scale degree in common, while the I and V triads share the 5th scale degree. When the 1st degree is the melody tone, the I or IV triads are the harmonic choices; the 5th scale degree may be harmonized by either the I or V triads. The I, IV, and V triads are known as the *tonic*, *subdominant*, and *dominant*, respectively.

EXAMPLE 9-2

a. Chord choices according to scale degree

Scale Degree in Melody	Choice of Triad	
1, 3, 5	I Triad	(Tonic)
4, 6, 1	IV Triad	(Subdominant)
5, 7, 2	V Triad	(Dominant)

b. Common tones between triads

    I   IV   I   V

The 7th scale degree (leading tone) has a strong tendency to progress to the 1st degree (tonic). Because it contains the 7th scale degree, the V triad is thus inclined to lead to the I triad, as shown in Example 9–3.

EXAMPLE 9–3

leading tone

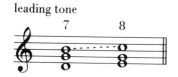

A comparison of *a* through *d* in Example 9–4 shows how triads built on the 4th and 5th scale degrees are used in melodic harmonization. The melody in Example 9–4*a* consists entirely of the 1st, 3rd, and 5th scale degrees in the key of G major. In *b*, the melody from *a* is harmonized with the I triad only. The embellishing tones added in *c* are then harmonized in *d*. (Note that harmonization of the 2nd, 4th, 6th, and 7th scale degrees requires the IV and V triads as well as the I.) Line *e* involves a more creative level of harmonization in which the composer or arranger selects the melody tones that are to be harmonized.

EXAMPLE 9–4

a. Simple melody with 1st, 3rd, and 5th scale degrees only

b. Melody in *a* harmonized with the I triad

c. Melody in *a* harmonized with the I triad (embellishing tones added)

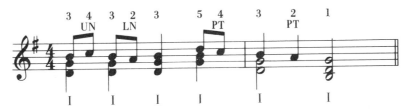

d. Melody in *a* with all embellishing tones harmonized (I, IV, and V triads required)

e. Melody in *a* with all triad tones harmonized (some embellishing tones harmonized)

Example 9–5 contains several possibilities for harmonizing various scale degrees with I, IV, and V triads. The 1st, 3rd, and 5th scale degrees are treated as principal tones. In *a*, the 1st scale degree is the principal melody tone; the tones G and E, which are the 2nd and 7th scale degrees and could be left as neighbor tones, are harmonized with the V triad. The I and V triads are incorporated into a sample harmonization in *b*. Some harmonic possibilities for the 5th and 3rd scale degrees and their neighbor tones are presented in *c* through *f*. Two systems for indicating harmony are given in Example 9–5*b*, *d*, and *f*. The letters above the staff tell the name of the chord (e.g., F, B♭, or C), the roman numerals (I, IV, or V) below the staff identify the scale degree on which the harmony is built.

EXAMPLE 9–5

a. 1st scale degree as principal melody tone

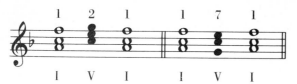

b. Sample harmonization

c. 5th scale degree as principal melody tone

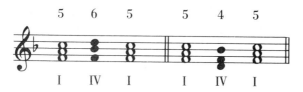

d. Sample harmonization

e. 3rd scale degree as principal melody tone

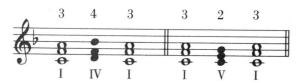

f. Sample harmonization

¶**EXERCISE 9-1**   After studying Examples 9–4 and 9–5, practice harmonizing the following melodic fragments in the right column. One of several possible harmonizations for each melody is given in the left column.

Answers

Harmonizing melodies

Bridge of Avignon

Meter

A second criterion for planning harmonic changes concerns the placement of tones on strong or weak beats within a melody. Although there are no hard and fast rules, the following general guidelines may be helpful:

1. Harmonies are usually placed on strong beats of the measure (see *beats* and *meter* in Chapter 1). In Example 9–6, scale degrees are harmonized on strong first beats.

EXAMPLE 9–6

EXAMPLE 9–7

2. Harmonies occurring on strong beats may be sustained from one beat up to an entire measure, or even more. In Example 9–7, the I triad is sustained for two measures, a total of six beats.

3. Harmonies on weak beats tend to sound as enrichments or embellishments of harmonies on strong beats and, therefore, are often not held longer than a single beat. In Example 9–8, the IV triad is not held beyond the weak beat. The V triad, placed on the strong first beat of measure 2, is sustained for three beats.

EXAMPLE 9–8

Tempo

A third criterion for making harmonic choices is *tempo*, or the speed at which a melody is to be performed. Compare the three harmonizations of the melody in Example 9–9*a*, *b*, and *c*. In *a* the tempo is slow, and every tone is harmonized. Because the more rapid tempo in *b* makes frequent changes of harmony more cumbersome, fewer harmonic changes are used. In the very fast tempo in *c*, even a single harmony sounds appropriate.

EXAMPLE 9–9

Other Considerations

Harmonizing melodies with I, IV, and V triads sometimes requires other special considerations:

1. The progression from V to IV is avoided in some styles. The progression from V to I is much stronger than from V to IV. Remember that the V triad contains the leading tone (LT), which has a tendency to pull toward the I. In Example 9–10, the progression on the staff below measure 2 may be preferable.

EXAMPLE 9–10

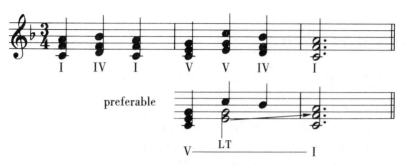

2. The progression from IV to V should be avoided in some styles if the melody ascends from the 1st to the 2nd scale degree, thus producing parallel 5ths (Ex. 9-11a). An undesirable progression may often be remedied by choosing an alternative chord (Ex. 9-11b). The progression from IV to V is a good choice, however, when the melody descends (Ex. 9-11c).

EXAMPLE 9-11

a. Parallel 5ths avoided in some musical styles

b. Undesirable parallel 5ths in *a* avoided by choosing a I chord instead of a IV for the second triad

c. IV to V progression used for descending melody

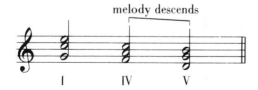

3. The progression from V to I (Ex. 9-12) is a very desirable one, especially between the two final chords in a melody.

EXAMPLE 9–12

I   V   I   IV   V   I

Harmonic Choices and Melodic Phrase

Because songs are based on language, they have phrase structures that closely resemble those of poetry. When setting words to music, composers usually build the "natural" pauses between phrases in the language into the music as well. Breaks in the musical flow are often marked with longer note values and rests which give the singer time to breathe. Composers can further control the feeling of a pause by deciding which scale tone will end the phrase. Melodic phrases ending on the tonic note have a relatively conclusive feel while those ending on any other tone, especially one in the V triad (5th, 7th, and 2nd degrees), are more dependent on a succeeding phrase.

The close bond between words and music is evident in "Old Folks at Home," Example 9–13. The first phrase of the words (meas. 1–4) seems incomplete and depends on the succeeding phrase (meas. 5–8) for the full

EXAMPLE 9–13

OLD FOLKS AT HOME

Stephen C. Foster

Way   down up - on the   Swa - nee Riv - er.   Far,   far   a - way

I   Antecedent Phrase   V

There's   where my heart is   turn - ing   ev - er,   There's where the old   folks   stay.

I   Consequent Phrase   I

meaning. Likewise, the first phrase of the musical setting of these words sounds inconclusive because it ends on D, the 2nd scale degree. If harmonic choices are limited to the I, IV, or V triads, a phrase ending on the 2nd scale degree must be harmonized with the V triad. Such a musical phrase, called an *antecedent phrase*, depends on the *consequent phrase* (meas. 5–8) for a more conclusive ending on the tonic note. An antecedent and consequent pair of phrases, such as that in the first eight measures of "Old Folks at Home," forms a larger formal unit called a *period*, or *sentence*.

Tonal contrast, which creates the anticipation of return, is one of the fundamentals for building musical compositions. The C tonality in this song is not destroyed by the 2nd scale degree at the beginning of measure 4, but is probably strengthened by the anticipation of an eventual return of the tonic in measure 8.

Phrases ending on the 5th scale degree offer the choice of harmonizing with either a I or a V triad. If the 5th degree at the end of an antecedent phrase is harmonized with the I chord, as in measure 12 of Example 9–14, however, the feeling of finality is somewhat weak. The antecedent phrase does not sound as though it should stand alone, yet its dependence on the consequent phrase does not seem as strong as that of an antecedent phrase ending on the V.

EXAMPLE 9–14

ONE MORE RIVER
(Noah's Ark)

EXAMPLE 9–15

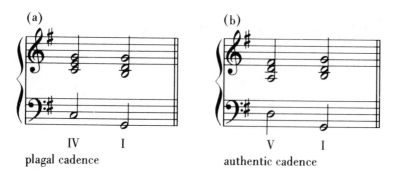

The chord progression at the end of a phrase is called a *cadence*. An antecedent phrase often ends with the inconclusive cadence I–V. The more conclusive consequent phrase sometimes ends with the IV–I, or *plagal* cadence (Ex. 9-15*a*), but most often with the V–I, generally known as an *authentic* cadence (Ex. 9-15*b*).

❡ **EXERCISE 9-2**   After studying the sample harmonization of the song "Annie Laurie" below, use I, IV, and V triads to harmonize the melodies in the right column. A possible harmonization of each melody is given in the left column.

Suggested study:
1. Determine the scale degree of each tone in the melody.
2. Refer to the summary of chord choices according to scale degree in Example 9–2*a* and *b*; then pencil in a preliminary harmonization.
3. Check tempo, meter, and rhythm. Using the guidelines set forth in Examples 9–6 through 9–12, make final decisions about which tones to harmonize and which to leave as embellishing tones.

ANNIE LAURIE

Answers | Harmonizing melodies

Angels We Have Heard on High

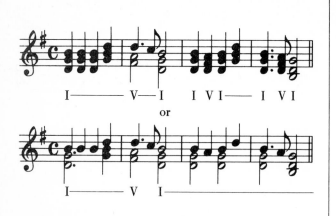

I———— V—I   I V I———— I V I

or

I———— V   I————————

Row, Row, Row Your Boat

I————————————————————

Battle Hymn of the Republic
William Steffe

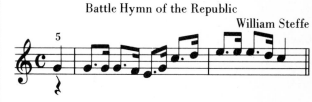

I   I   I   I   I   I V I

I———— IV   I   V   I

I   V   I   V   I   IV V I V   I

Harmonizing in Four Parts

All of the harmonizations in previous sections involve three parts, or triads. Four-part harmony, which is typically found in choral music, accommodates the four ranges of human singing voices: soprano, alto, tenor, and bass (Ex. 9-16*a*). Another common four-part arrangement is keyboard style (Ex. 9-16*b*). Although *a* and *b* involve the same pitches, their formats differ. One way to expand three-part harmony into four parts is to double the *root* of the triad.

EXAMPLE 9–16

(a) Four-part chorale style

(b) Four-part keyboard style

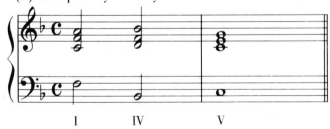

Determining the Root of a Triad

The *root* is the scale degree upon which the triad is built:

1. The root of the I triad is the 1st degree of the scale.
2. The root of the IV triad is the 4th degree of the scale.
3. The root of the V triad is the 5th degree of the scale.

In a harmonization the tones of each triad are arranged to accommodate the tones of the melody. The three possible positions of the C-major triad are shown in Example 9–17a. A melodic fragment is harmonized with the C-major triad in Example 9–17b.

EXAMPLE 9–17

(a) The three triad positions

(b) The three triad positions in a typical harmonization

EXAMPLE 9–18

If the root is the lowest tone of a triad, that triad is in *root position* (Ex. 9-18). The root is the only tone of the triad that, when placed on the bottom, will allow the remainder of the triad to be spelled in *thirds*. Notice that the root of the triad in Example 9–19 is F.

EXAMPLE 9–19

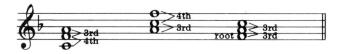

◀ EXERCISE 9-3   Circle the root of each triad in the right column. Refer to Examples 9–18 and 9–19 if necessary. Check answers in the left column.

Answers	Finding Triad Roots

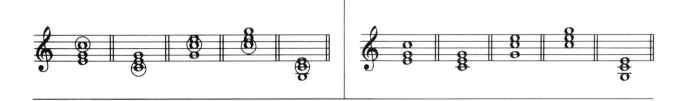

Converting Three-part Harmony to Four Parts

The three positions of the G-major triad in Example 9–20a are converted to four-part harmonies in Example 9–20b by doubling the root. The lowest sounding voice always determines the position of any chord, regardless of what is in the upper three voices. If the root of a chord is the lowest voice, the chord is in *root position*. All of the four-part chords in Example 9–20b are in root position. As shown in Example 9–20c, four-part chords may also be in *first inversion* (the 3rd of the chord is the lowest tone) or *second inversion* (the 5th of the chord is the lowest tone). All harmonies in the following exercises will be limited to root position.

EXAMPLE 9–20

(a) Three-part harmony

(b) Four-part harmony (keyboard style)

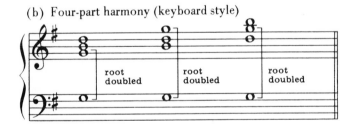

(c) Chord Inversions

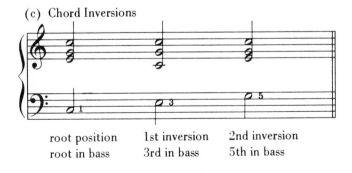

root position   1st inversion   2nd inversion
root in bass   3rd in bass   5th in bass

◖EXERCISE 9-4   Convert each triad in the right column into four parts by doubling the root. Check answers in the left column.

Answers   Writing four-part chords

¶EXERCISE 9-5   Expand the following progressions into four parts by doubling the root of each triad. Write chord symbols under each progression. Check answers in the left column.

Answers

Writing progressions

❈EXERCISE 9-6   Harmonize each melodic fragment in the right column with I, IV, and V chords in four-part keyboard style. Remember that some tones may be treated as embellishing tones and need not be harmonized. Suggested harmonizations are provided in the left column.

Answers   Harmonizing melodies

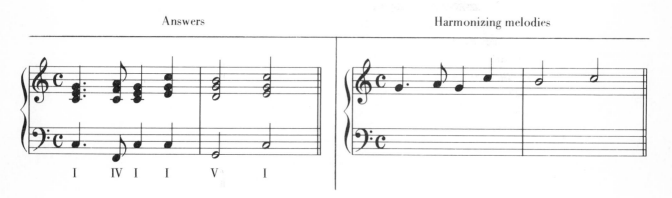

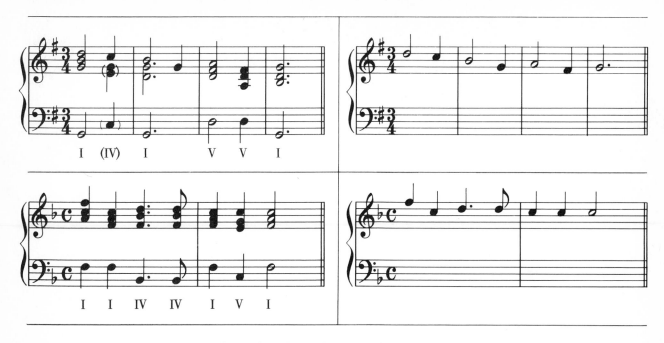

Using I, IV, and V chords in keyboard style, harmonize the following familiar melodies:

ODE TO JOY

Ludwig van Beethoven, Symphony No. 9

DECK THE HALLS

Welsh

JINGLE BELLS

Harmonizing with the V⁷ Chord

The *dominant 7th chord* is created by adding a 3rd on top of a V triad, as in Example 9–21*a* and *b*. Because this additional 3rd is the interval of a 7th above the root of the V triad, the new chord is called a dominant 7th, or V⁷. For ease in identification, the 7th is represented with a black notehead in Examples 9–21 through 9–26. In Example 9–22*a* and *b*, compare the V chord positions with the V⁷ chord positions. Notice that the four voices of the V⁷ allow a third inversion.

EXAMPLE 9–21

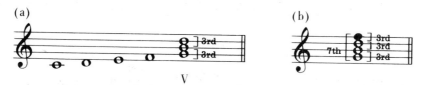

Although the V⁷ is a four-part chord, it may be reduced to fewer voices with no loss of harmonic effectiveness. In Example 9–22*c*, the V⁷ is reduced to three voices by eliminating either the 5th or the 3rd of the chord; the 5th is the preferred omission unless it is the melody tone. Except when the 5th is in the top voice, even a two-voice structure carries the full implication of the V⁷ chord (Ex. 9-22*d*). In each case, the 7th plus either the root or the 3rd will represent the V⁷ quality—as in the familiar "Chopsticks." Example 9–23*a* contains the first few measures of this song; *b* is a reduction which shows the harmony without rhythm, while *c* gives the full implied harmonies.

The V⁷ offers more possibilities for harmonizing melodies than the V triad for two reasons: (1) It may be used to harmonize the 4th scale degree as well as the 5th, 7th, and 2nd degrees, and (2) it has a stronger attraction

EXAMPLE 9–22

(a) Positions of the V triad

melody tone

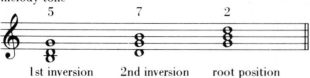

1st inversion   2nd inversion   root position

(b) Positions of the V7 chord

melody tone

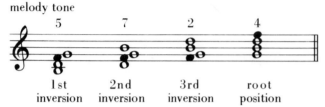

1st inversion   2nd inversion   3rd inversion   root position

(c) V7 reduced to three voices

(d) V7 reduced to two voices

EXAMPLE 9–23

(a)

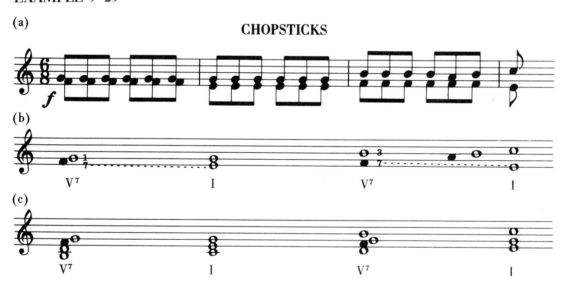

CHOPSTICKS

(b)

V⁷   I   V⁷   I

(c)

V⁷   I   V⁷   I

to the I triad. Compare the harmonization of the scale degrees 5–4–3–2–1 using the I, IV, and V triads only (Ex. 9–24a) with alternatives involving the V⁷ chord (Ex. 9–24b and c).

Traditionally, the 7th of the V⁷ chord (4th scale degree) moves downward to the 3rd scale degree in the progression V⁷–I. As indicated

EXAMPLE 9–24

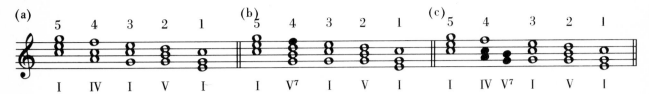

with dotted lines in Example 9–25, the combination of the downward motion of its 7th (4th scale degree) and the upward motion of its 3rd (leading tone) gives the V⁷ chord a strong attraction to the I triad.

EXAMPLE 9–25

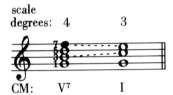

In the typical V⁷–I progressions in Example 9–26a, observe the melody tones that may be harmonized with the V⁷. Note also the strong tendency of the 3rd and 7th of the V⁷ to resolve; even with the remaining tones eliminated, as in Example 9–26b, V⁷–I progressions are still implied. In Example 9–26c, the V⁷ is shown in keyboard style.

EXAMPLE 9–26

❰**EXERCISE 9-7** Using Example 9–26 as a guide, convert the V chords to V⁷ chords in the following progressions in keyboard style. When the 7th is added, eliminate the appropriate tone to maintain only three upper voices. A possible solution for each is given in the left column.

Answers

Writing V7 chords

Harmonize the following melodic fragments. Use V⁷ chords whenever appropriate. Possible solutions are given in the left column.

Answers　　　　　　　　　　　　　　　　　Harmonizing melodies

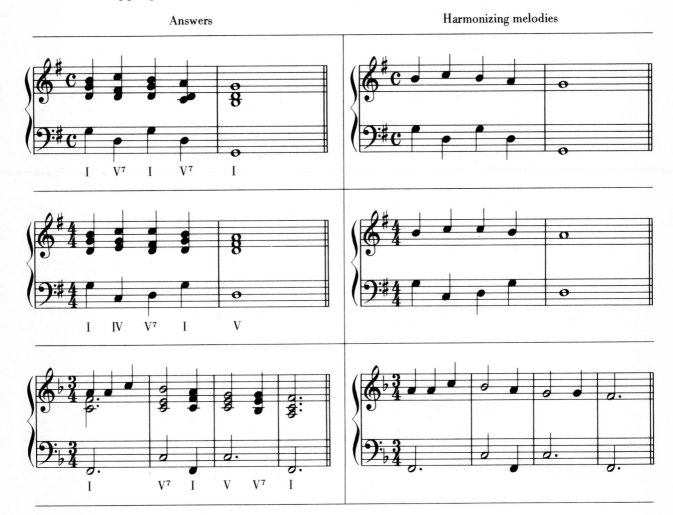

Harmonizing Melodies in Three Common Minor Keys

The principles for harmonizing melodies in major keys apply to harmonizing melodies in minor keys as well. Remember, however, that in minor keys the leading tone (7th scale degree) is often raised, depending upon the form of the scale. The V and V⁷ chords in harmonizations in this section will reflect that alteration, as shown in Example 9–27. (For a review of minor scales, refer to Chapter 7.)

EXAMPLE 9–27

* Raised 7th scale degree

❪EXERCISE 9-8   Using Example 9–27 as a guide, harmonize the following melodies in minor keys. Suggested harmonizations are given in the left column.

Suggested harmonizations   Harmonizing minor melodies

Harmonize the following familiar melody in E minor. A possible harmonization is given immediately following the song.

JOSHUA FOUGHT THE BATTLE OF JERICHO

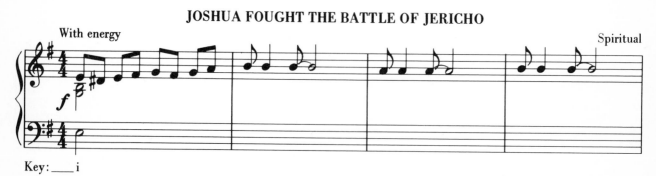

Key:____ i

Possible harmonization:

JOSHUA FOUGHT THE BATTLE OF JERICHO

CHAPTER TEN
Tonality as an Organizing Force

The ability to create anticipation in the listener is one of the successful composer's most powerful tools. In Chapter 9 you saw how a composer can build expectation into the music by ending an antecedent phrase with a tone other than the tonic. Such an antecedent phrase seems to call for a consequent phrase with a more conclusive ending. This tonal contrast between individual phrases significantly affects the listener's reaction to a piece of music. One way to emphasize the nontonic ending of an antecedent phrase is to use a *secondary leading tone*.

Secondary Leading Tones

From Chapter 9, recall the special function of the leading tone (7th scale degree) and its usual progression upward $\frac{1}{2}$-step to the tonic. This half-step relationship between the leading tone and the tonic can be transferred to other scale degrees by means of accidentals. In Example 10–1a, the dominant tone G (5th degree) at the end of the antecedent phrase in measure 4 is emphasized by the half-step progression from the F♯ (raised 4th scale degree). Functioning as a leading tone to the dominant tone G, the F♯ is a *secondary leading tone* in the key of C major. In Example 10–1b, in F major, the B♮ in measure 4 is the secondary leading tone to the

EXAMPLE 10–1

(a)

STAR-SPANGLED BANNER

Francis Scott Key

Stafford Smith

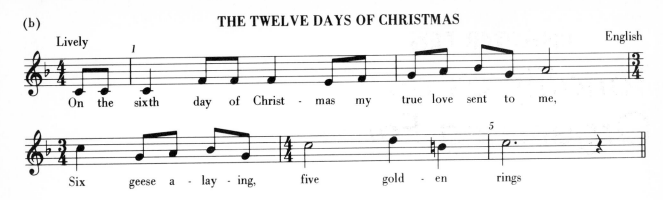

(b)

THE TWELVE DAYS OF CHRISTMAS

English

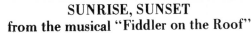

SUNRISE, SUNSET
from the musical "Fiddler on the Roof"

Words by Sheldon Harnick

Music by Jerry Bock

dominant tone C in measure 5. Leading tones and secondary leading tones are found in "Sunrise, Sunset," in G minor (Ex. 10–1c). The F♯'s are raised leading tones in the G harmonic minor scale (meas. 2, 6, 18, and 22 of the excerpt). The B♮ in measure 26 and the C♯ in measure 28 are both secondary leading tones in the key of G minor. The B♮ leads to the C in the following measure, while the C♯ leads to the D in measure 29.

Secondary Dominants

If a secondary leading tone in a melody is harmonized, the resultant chord is a *secondary dominant*. Compare the V–I progression in Example 10–2*a* with the V of V (V/V) in *b*. In the reduction beneath *b*, notice that the F♯ is the 3rd of the D-major triad, which is the dominant of G, or

EXAMPLE 10–2

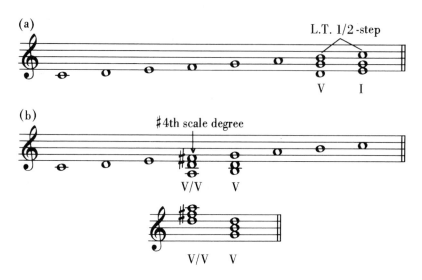

V/V in C major. Any tone that is raised with an accidental can act as a secondary leading tone and thus as the 3rd of a secondary dominant chord. The strength of the V–I progression, then, may be shifted temporarily to the dominant by using the secondary dominant (V/V). In Example 10–3, the V/V before the V harmony at the end of the antecedent phrase in measure 4 heightens the anticipation of the return of the I in the consequent phrase.

EXAMPLE 10–3

STAR-SPANGLED BANNER

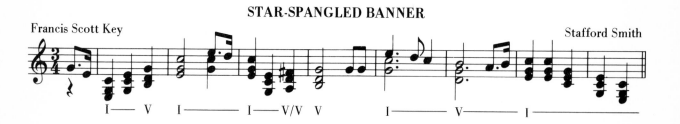

Although the raised 4th scale degree in a melody indicates a possible secondary dominant, other tones of the V/V (2nd and 6th degrees) are often harmonized as well. Example 10–4 shows other melody tones that are frequently harmonized with the secondary dominant.

EXAMPLE 10–4

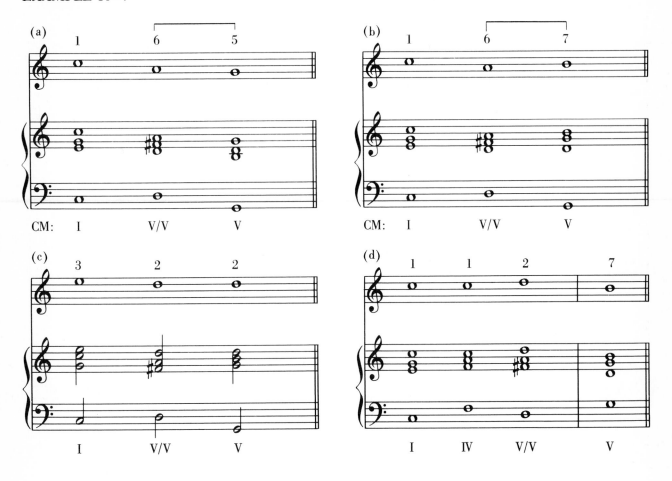

❰EXERCISE 10–1   Write a secondary dominant (V/V) before the V chord near the end of each phrase. Remember that a raised 4th scale degree in the melody may be treated as the *3rd* of the V/V chord. Check suggested solutions in the left column.

Answers   Writing secondary dominants

Chord Progressions Around the Circle of Fifths

The secondary dominant is used in more extensive chord progressions such as the common V/V–V–I. In the key of C major, this progression involves the D, G, and C triads with roots one 5th apart (Ex. 10-5).

EXAMPLE 10–5

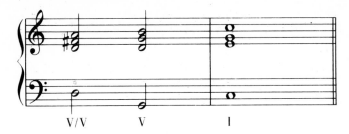

V/V   V   I

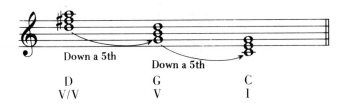

Down a 5th

Down a 5th

D   G   C
V/V   V   I

Study the chord root relationships in the circle of fifths in Example 10–6. A succession of chords with roots a 5th apart underlies much music and is especially noticeable in popular and jazz styles, which often have bass lines moving in 4ths and 5ths. In measures 41 to 48 of the well-known song "Sunrise, Sunset" (Ex. 10-7), the harmonic progression, indicated by letter symbols above the melodic line, moves through two segments of the circle of fifths. Disregarding 7ths and chord qualities, the roots of the progression are as follows: C–F–B♭–A–D–G. Reading counterclockwise on the circle of fifths in Example 10–6, find this progression. Notice that with the exception of the B♭ to A, each succeeding chord in this series is one 5th lower. Although it is possible to go around the entire circle in this way, composers usually interrupt the progression and include only a few such chords at one time.

EXAMPLE 10–6

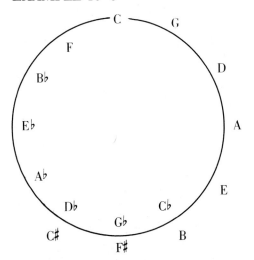

Many compositions contain progressions that extend at least partially around the circle of fifths. However, bass lines usually do not move in a

EXAMPLE 10–7

SUNRISE, SUNSET
from the musical "Fiddler on the Roof"

Words by Sheldon Harnick

Music by Jerry Bock

continuous string of 5ths like the one in Example 10–8*a*. The more practical zigzag pattern, down a 5th and up a 4th (Ex. 10–8*b*), keeps the tones in a narrow range while maintaining the impact of the circle of fifths progression. This reliance on intervals of 4ths and 5ths gives bass lines in popular music much of their power and appeal.

EXAMPLE 10–8

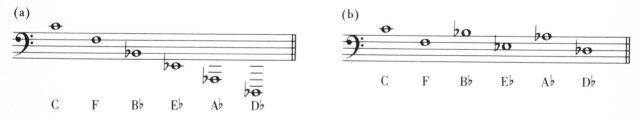

To determine the tones of a bass line in a circle of fifths progression, follow these steps:

1. Choose a key and write its scale in descending order. As indicated with brackets, number the first four tones with odd numbers and the next four with even numbers.

2. Place the second bracket beneath the first so that the scale tones alternate in a zigzag fashion (down a 5th and up a 4th).

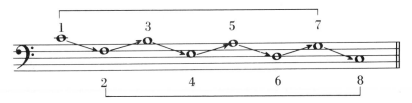

A full four-part harmonization of the circle of fifths progression in C major is given in Example 10–9. Unless altered with accidentals, the harmony on the 7th degree of the major scale is a diminished chord (vii°). You may notice some discrepancy between the letter names on the circle of fifths in Example 10–6 and those in the bass line of Example 10–9.

EXAMPLE 10–9

EXAMPLE 10–10

Following the circle of fifths exactly, the succession of roots should be C-F-B♭-E♭-A♭, and so on. Remember, however, that the key of C major has no sharps or flats in its key signature. The circle of fifths progression, then, conforms to the letter names in the circle of fifths, but the accidentals are dependent on the key signature. Bass lines for the keys of F major and G major are given in Example 10–10*a* and *b*.

Modulation

Tonal contrast in a composition may be expanded to the extent that entire sections are in keys different from the one at the beginning. Invariably, however, such a composition is rounded off by a return to the original key. This process of changing keys is called *modulation*. In major keys, the most common modulation shifts the tonality from the tonic to the dominant; in minor, the most common modulation is from the tonic to the relative major.

One of the chief ways to modulate from one key to another is through a *secondary dominant*. In such a modulation, the secondary dominant in the old key is interpreted as the dominant (V) of the new key. Often, however, a shift of tonality is so brief that it is difficult to determine if a modulation has occurred. "O Come, All Ye Faithful" (Ex. 10-11) achieves much of its vitality from the tonal contrasts between the beginnings and endings of its five phrases. Although all phrases begin on the tonic, G, the first four end on the dominant, D. The final phrase, ending in G major, supplies the appropriate feeling of completeness for the entire song.

EXAMPLE 10–11

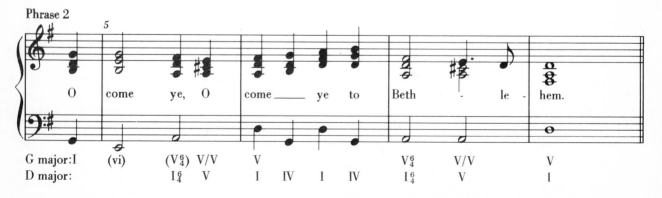

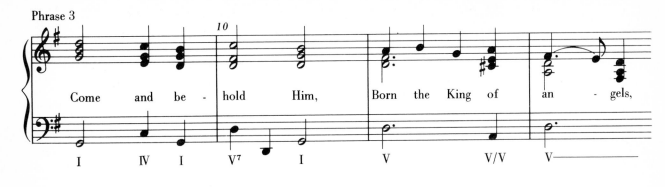

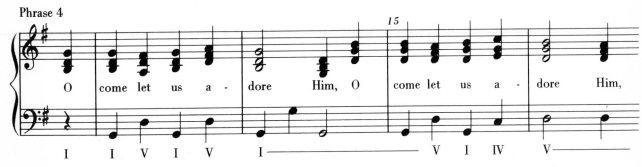

If you examine "O Come, All Ye Faithful," you will find that two of its phrases contain secondary dominants. Phrase 1 ends on the dominant chord, but no secondary dominant is employed. Phrase 2, however, has a much more extensive emphasis of the V tonality. The V/V in measure 5 sets up the V chord, which is expanded throughout measure 6 and strengthened by a second V/V in measure 7. In addition, the whole note in measure 8 further emphasizes the D-major tonality. The upper line of chord symbols indicates that although this phrase involves secondary dominants, it remains in the original key of G major. The lower line of symbols, on the other hand, interprets this phrase as a brief modulation to the key of D major, the dominant of G major. The dominant chord at the end of phrase 3 is preceded by its dominant, or the V/V; nevertheless, this phrase does not have the strong feeling of modulation that phrase 2 had. Although phrase 4 ends on the dominant chord, no secondary dominant is involved. Phrase 5 has a firm ending on the tonic chord, G major.

Sometimes it is difficult to decide whether a chord is a secondary dominant in the old key or the dominant in a new key. One factor to consider is the length of time that a new tonality is emphasized or confirmed in a composition. Because so much time is devoted to the dominant harmony in phrase 2 of "O Come, All Ye Faithful," the D-major tonality becomes a rival with the original key of G major as the principal key. Notice, however, that phrase 3 begins in the old key of G major—thus diminishing the idea that phrase 2 is anything more than a brief expansion of the dominant of the original key.

Modulations are more easily defined in longer musical forms where sufficient time can be devoted to confirming new tonalities. In Example 10–12, the *Sonatine* begins in the key of G major but cadences in the dominant, D major, at the double bar in measure 22. To discover how this modulation is produced, locate the C♯ in measure 7. As shown on the staff beneath measure 7, this C♯ is the 3rd of the A-major chord, or the V/V in G major. If you look forward in the music, however, you will see that the progression between the A-major chord and the D-major chord is repeated so many times that D major is established as the new key at the double bar in measure 22. What at first appeared to be the V/V in G major is really the V chord in the new key of D major.

EXAMPLE 10–12

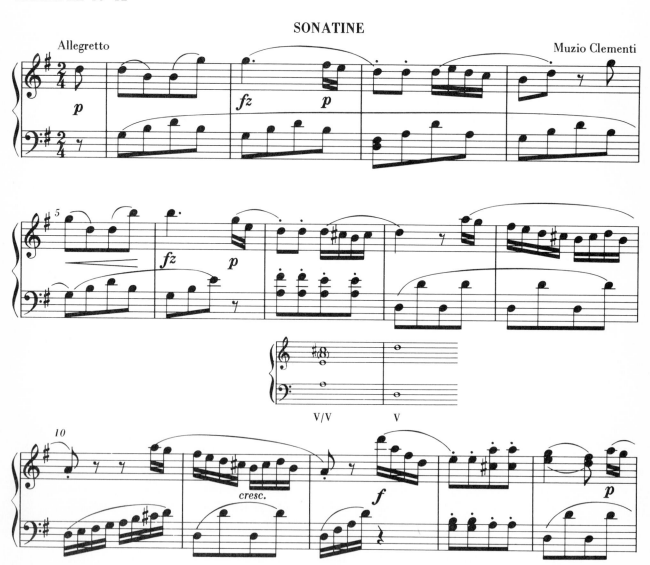

SONATINE

Allegretto

Muzio Clementi

V/V   V

CHAPTER ELEVEN
Other Scales
and Triad Qualities

Modes

The major and minor scales, or *modes*, studied in earlier chapters are not the only tonal resources available to composers. Before 1600, a system of modal scales (from which the major and minor scales developed) was the basis of Western music, but between 1600 and 1900, the major and minor modes gained favor. Compositions by famous composers such as Bach, Haydn, Mozart, and Beethoven were usually written in either major or minor keys. Only in church music and folk music did the modes continue as a tradition. In the late 1800s, folk music, which often employs modes other than major and minor, became a frequent source of inspiration for compositions. Although the major and minor modes are the primary means for tonal organization in music today, continued interest in folk music has caused a resurgence of the other modes.

Each of the modes, sometimes called the *church modes*, has a unique pattern of whole and half steps. The *Ionian* and the *Aeolian* modes correspond to the major scale and the minor scale, respectively. (Refer to Chapter 3 for major scales and Chapter 7 for minor scales, if necessary.) Recall that each minor key has a relative major key with the same key signature. For example, A minor and its relative major, C major, are scales that share the key signature of no sharps or flats (Ex. 11-1). The

EXAMPLE 11–1

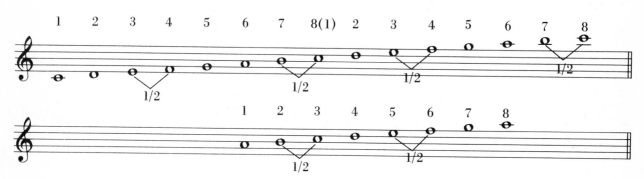

172

pattern of whole and half steps for the A-minor scale is produced by starting on the 6th degree of C major.

As you can see in Box 11–1, C major and A minor are only two of the scale patterns possible with the key signature of no sharps or flats. Five other modes on white keys only also share that same key signature. While the C-major scale *does not* generate the other modal scales in any way, it is convenient to think of it as the starting point for calculating where to write the other modes. By starting scales on different intervals above C, you can create the unique pattern of whole and half steps for each mode. To make your work with modes easier, *memorize* the relationships on white keys only in Box 11–1. Later in this chapter, you will learn how to determine modes with other key signatures.

BOX 11–1

On the white keys only of the keyboard (no sharps or flats), the following relationships exist between the C-major scale and the other modes:

1. The *Ionian* mode, identical to the major scale, occurs between C and C.

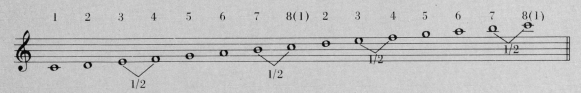

2. The *Dorian* mode is built on the 2nd scale degree (from D to D).

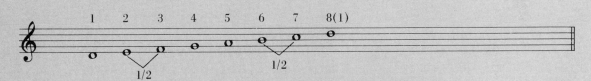

3. The *Phrygian* mode is built on the 3rd scale degree (from E to E).

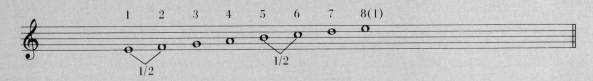

4. The *Lydian* mode is built on the 4th scale degree (from F to F).

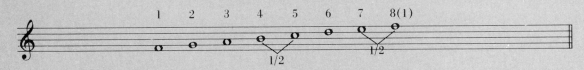

5. The *Mixolydian* mode is built on the 5th scale degree (from G to G).

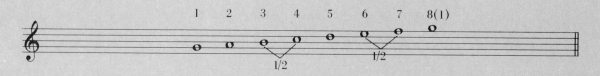

6. The *Aeolian* mode, identical to the minor scale, is built on the 6th scale degree (from A to A).

7. The *Locrian* mode, not an original church mode, refers to the pattern beginning on the 7th scale degree (from B to B).

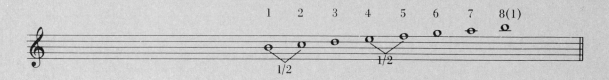

Like major and minor scales, the modes can be transposed to other tonal levels. Each major key signature, then, is shared by a group of modal scales with an identical set of relationships to those in Box 11–1. To determine the key or mode of a composition, you must compare the key signature with the scale on which the music is based. The key in Example 11–2a is F major because the key signature has one flat and the melody is based on the scale from F to F. Remember that this melody may also be termed *Ionian*, the mode identical to the major scale.

EXAMPLE 11–2

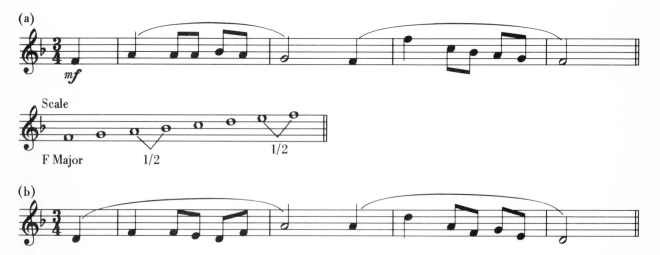

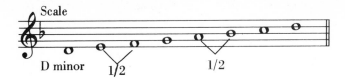

Although the key signature in Example 11–2b is also the same as F major, the melody is based on a scale from D to D, the relative minor of F major. This melody, then, is in the key of D minor, or the *Aeolian* mode on D. The mode upon which any composition is based may be determined by the key signature/scale comparison.

The melody in Example 11–3a is in the *Dorian* mode; the key signature is that of F major, but the scale lies between G and G, the 2nd scale degree of F major. (Remember from Box 11–1 that the Dorian mode pattern may be built by starting on the 2nd degree of a major scale.) Although the key signature in Example 11–3b is again that of F major, the "tonic" is really B♭, the 4th scale degree of F major. This melody is in the *Lydian* mode.

EXAMPLE 11–3

The key signature in Example 11–4 has two sharps (the key signature for D major), but the tonic is A—the 5th scale degree of D major. This melody, then, is in the *Mixolydian* mode.

Sharps or flats that determine the mode are not always written in the key signature but may sometimes occur as accidentals throughout a piece. For instance, the melody in Example 11–5 has the accidental F♯ written throughout. The fact that the F♯'s are all written as accidentals instead of in a key signature does not change the mode. Notice that the melody in Example 11–5 is based on a scale from B to B. Because B is the 3rd scale degree of the scale having one sharp in its key signature, G major, this

EXAMPLE 11–4

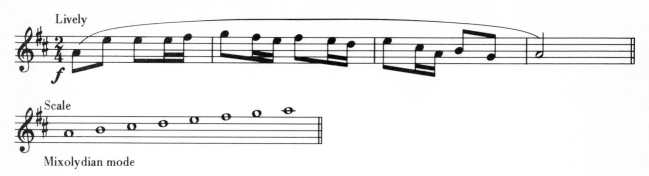

Mixolydian mode

EXAMPLE 11–5

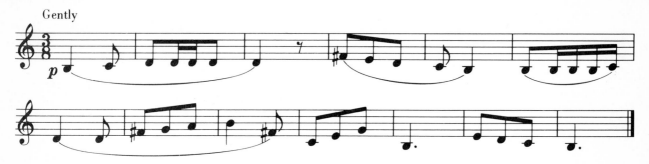

melody is in the *Phrygian* mode. The pattern of a scale may also be determined by the combination of a key signature and accidentals written in the melody.

Another way to explain the modes is to group them according to their similarities to the major or the minor scale:

Major scale	*Minor scale*
Ionian mode	Aeolian mode
Same as the major scale	Same as the minor scale
Lydian mode	Dorian mode
Like the major scale with the 4th degree raised	Like the minor scale with the 6th degree raised
Mixolydian mode	Phrygian mode
Like the major scale with the 7th degree lowered	Like the minor scale with the 2nd degree lowered

❰EXERCISE 11-1　After studying Examples 11–1 through 11–5 and Box 11–1, identify the following modes. Check your answers in the left column.

Suggested procedure for identifying modes:
1. Decide which major key is represented by the key signature.
2. Determine the tones of the scale (for example, D to D).
3. Determine which degree of the major scale the modal scale begins on.
4. Name the mode.

Major key signature = G major
Modal scale = D to D
Degree of major scale = 5th
Name of mode = Mixolydian

Answers	Identifying modes
Mixolydian	
Dorian	
Lydian	
Dorian	
Mixolydian	
Phrygian	
Dorian	
Aeolian	
Dorian	

Mixolydian	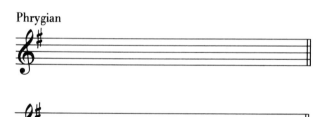

❰EXERCISE 11-2   Write the following modal scales. Check your answers in the left column.

Suggested procedure for writing modal scales:
1. Decide which major key is represented by the key signature.
2. Determine which degree of the major scale the modal scale will begin on.
3. Write the modal scale.

Major key signature = G major
Degree of major scale = 3rd
Modal scale = B to B

Phrygian

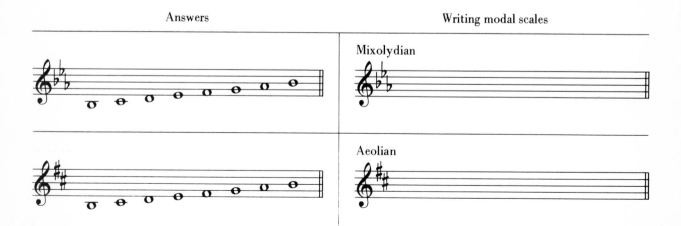

Answers	Writing modal scales

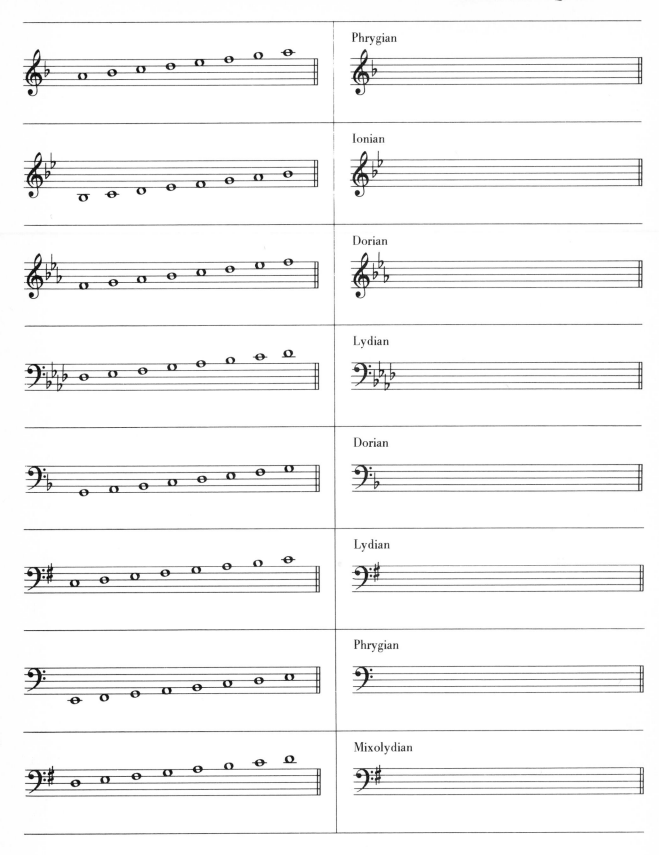

The Pentatonic Scale

Pentatonic scales are composed of five tones within the octave. Because the most common examples of these scales have no half steps (Ex. 11-6*a* and *b*), they lack the tonal focus created by the leading-tone resolution in a major scale. Instead, a tone usually assumes the role of tonic merely through repetition or rhythmic stress. Without the obligation to resolve leading tones, composers can use pitches in the pentatonic scale in any sequence with equally good results. This freedom in tonal organization also makes the pentatonic scale attractive for improvising, especially in folk music.

EXAMPLE 11–6

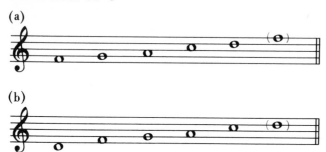

EXAMPLE 11–7

CINDY

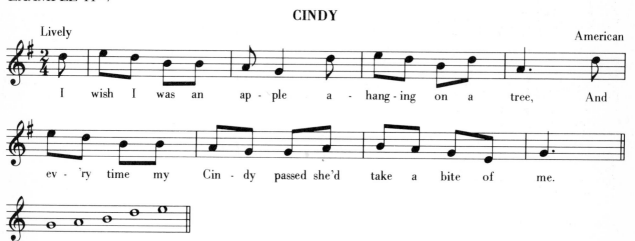

In "Cindy" (Ex. 11-7), notice the shift of the pentatonic scale on G to a lower pitch range in the chorus. Observe also the shift in range of the pentatonic scale in "Coffee Grows on White Oak Trees" (Ex. 11-8). "Get on Board" (Ex. 11-9) is another well-known pentatonic song.

EXAMPLE 11–8

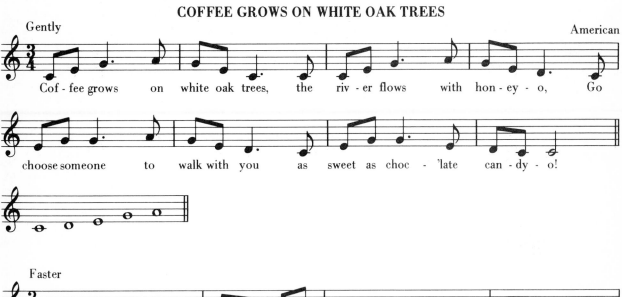

COFFEE GROWS ON WHITE OAK TREES

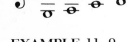

EXAMPLE 11–9

GET ON BOARD

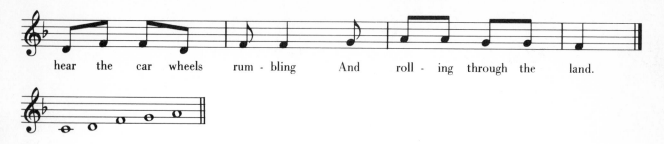

hear   the   car   wheels   rum - bling   And   roll - ing   through   the   land.

The Whole-tone Scale

The *whole-tone* scale is composed entirely of whole steps (Ex. 11-10*a* and *b*). With the absence of half steps, no leading tone is present to establish a clearcut tonality. Because of its tonal ambiguity, the whole-tone scale lacks the sense of direction and organizing power of the major and minor scales. Normally, only portions of a composition are based on the whole-tone scale.

EXAMPLE 11–10

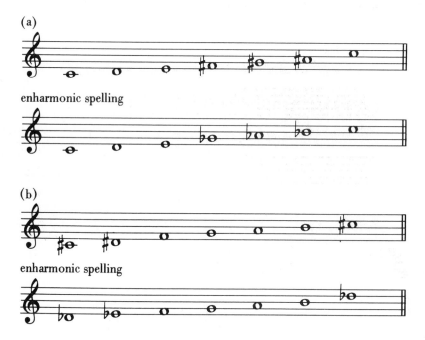

Triad Qualities

In previous chapters, major and minor triads were introduced with the study of major and minor keys. These triads, along with other triad qualities, will be studied in more detail in this section.

Triads consist of various combinations of major and minor 3rds. For easy reference, the major and minor 3rds possible on white keys of the keyboard are given in Example 11–11. (If necessary, review the characteristics of major and minor 3rds in Box 6–1).

EXAMPLE 11–11

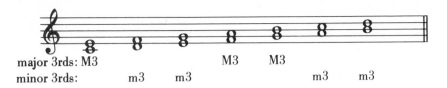

major 3rds: M3
minor 3rds:

Triad Qualities in Major Keys

If you build a triad above each tone of the C-major scale, you will see the three triad qualities possible on white keys only:

1. Major (major 3rd on the bottom and minor 3rd on top), Example 11–12*a*, built above the tones C, F, and G;
2. Minor (minor 3rd on the bottom and major 3rd on top), Example 11–12*b*, built above the tones D, E, and A;
3. Diminished (minor 3rds on both top and bottom), Example 11–12*c*, built on the tone B.

EXAMPLE 11–12

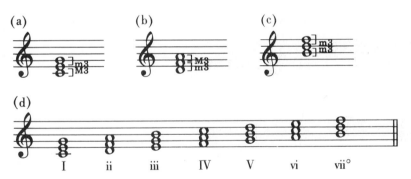

(a)   (b)   (c)

(d)

I   ii   iii   IV   V   vi   vii°

As shown in Example 11–12*d*, major triads are indicated by uppercase roman numerals, while minor and diminished triads are designated by lowercase roman numerals. The symbol for the diminished triad also contains a superscript, as in vii°.

The effects of adding accidentals to the triads in Example 11–12 are summarized in Box 11–2. As you will recall from Chapter 6, you may add like accidentals to both tones of an interval without changing its quality. Similarly, adding like accidentals to all three members of a triad does not alter its quality either.

In each section of the box, you will notice a fourth triad quality—*augmented*. Consisting of two major 3rds, the augmented triad requires at least one accidental.

BOX 11–2

The following major triads are possible on
white keys only of the keyboard:

Major triads

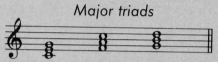

Adding like accidentals to all three members
of a major triad does not change its quality.

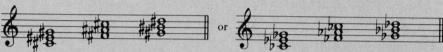

Adding the following accidentals changes the
quality of the above major triads:

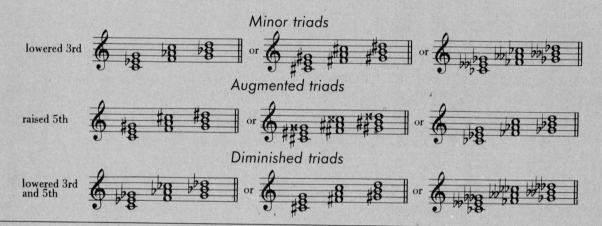

Minor triads

lowered 3rd

Augmented triads

raised 5th

Diminished triads

lowered 3rd
and 5th

The following minor triads are possible on
white keys only of the keyboard:

Minor triads

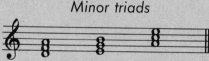

Adding like accidentals to all three members
of a minor triad does not change its quality.

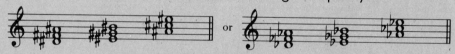

Adding the following accidentals changes
the quality of the above minor triads:

Major triads

raised 3rd

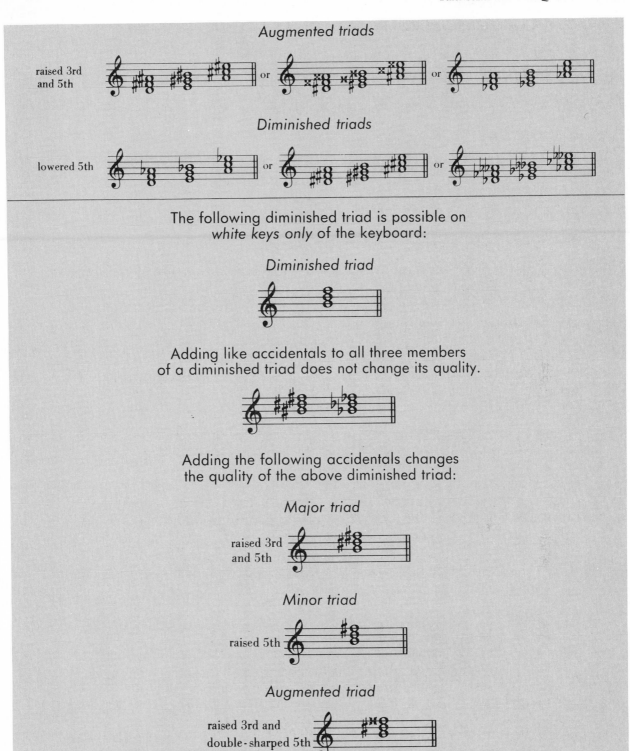

Augmented triads

raised 3rd and 5th

Diminished triads

lowered 5th

The following diminished triad is possible on
white keys only of the keyboard:

Diminished triad

Adding like accidentals to all three members
of a diminished triad does not change its quality.

Adding the following accidentals changes
the quality of the above diminished triad:

Major triad

raised 3rd
and 5th

Minor triad

raised 5th

Augmented triad

raised 3rd and
double-sharped 5th

The triad qualities shown in Example 11–12 using the tones of the
C-major scale are present in all other major keys as well. Example 11–
13*a* and *b* shows these triads built on the scale tones of two other common keys—F major and G major.

EXAMPLE 11–13

(a)

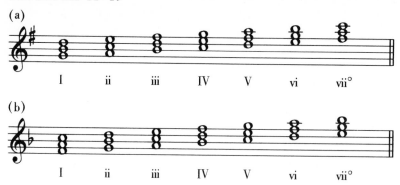

I   ii   iii   IV   V   vi   vii°

(b)

I   ii   iii   IV   V   vi   vii°

Triad Qualities in Minor Keys

Major, minor, and diminished triad qualities also occur in minor keys but are located on different scale degrees from those of the major keys (Ex. 11-14). As in the major scale, triad qualities are determined by the location of the whole and half steps. In the natural minor scale, triads built on the 1st, 4th, and 5th scale degrees are minor, triads on the 3rd, 6th, and 7th degrees are major, and the triad on the 2nd degree is diminished.

EXAMPLE 11–14

i   ii°   III   iv   v   VI   VII

In melodic minor scales, the 6th and 7th degrees are raised when the melody ascends to the tonic. The harmonic minor always has a raised 7th degree. (If necessary, review minor scales in Chapter 7.) Observe the variant triad qualities that result when these degrees are altered (Ex. 11-15). Note that "°" and "+" superscripts designate diminished and augmented chord qualities, respectively.

EXAMPLE 11–15

natural minor scale

unaltered triads: i   ii°   III   iv   v   VI   VII

melodic minor scale

altered triads: i   ii   III+   IV   V   ♮vi°   vii°

harmonic minor scale

altered triads: i   ii°   III+   iv   V   VI   vii°

◖EXERCISE 11-3 After studying Examples 11–11 through 11–15 and Box 11–2, write the following triads above the given tones. Check your answers in the left column.

Answers   Writing triad qualities

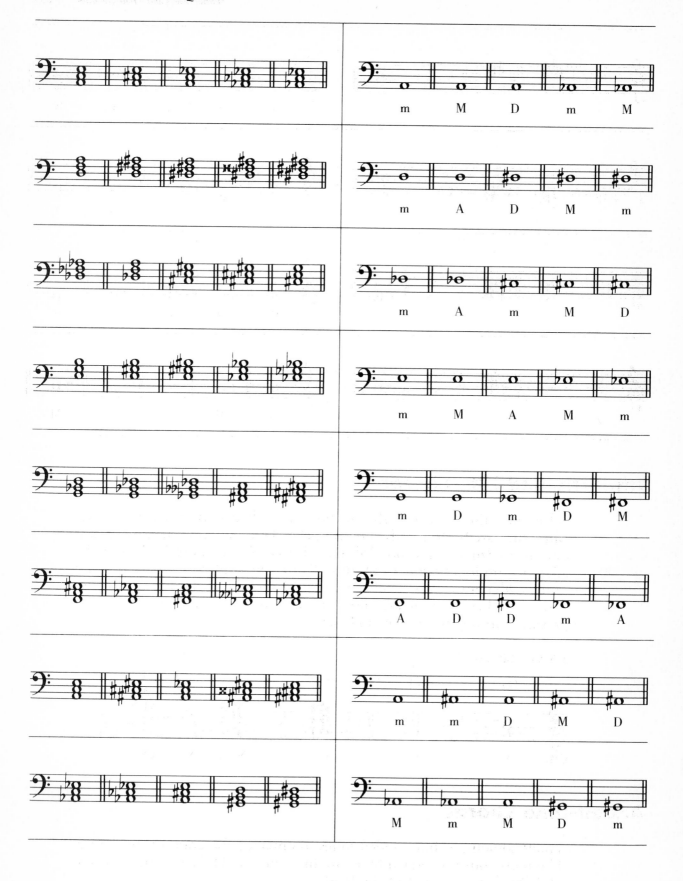

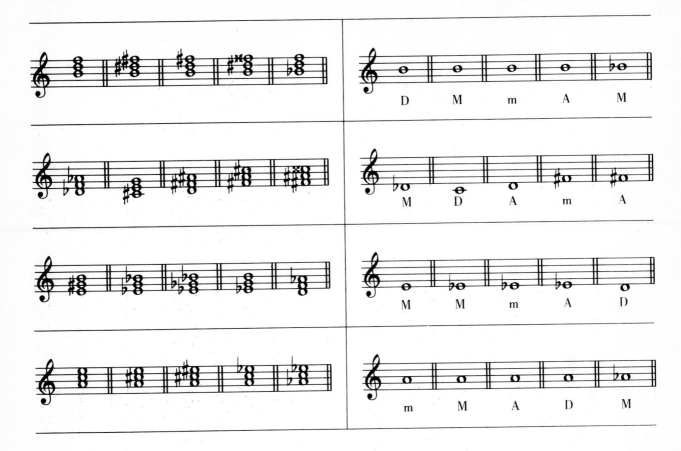

9th, 11th, and 13th Chords

All chords discussed in earlier sections are called *tertian* harmonies because they are built in 3rds. For example, the G-major triad is composed of a major 3rd and a minor 3rd (Ex. 11-16a). A 7th chord is obtained by adding a 3rd to a triad (Ex. 11-16b). By stacking additional 3rds, you can build a 9th chord, an 11th chord, or a 13th chord (Ex. 11-16c through e). Although these chords are found in several styles, they are especially prevalent in popular music and jazz.

EXAMPLE 11–16

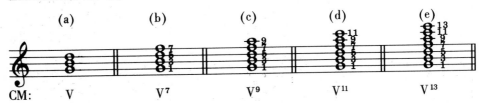

Added-tone Chords

Triads sometimes have added tones to enhance the color of the sound. The most common added tones are the 2nd (Ex. 11-17a) or the 6th (Ex. 11-17b) above the root of the triad.

EXAMPLE 11–17

(a) Added 2nd

(b) Added 6th

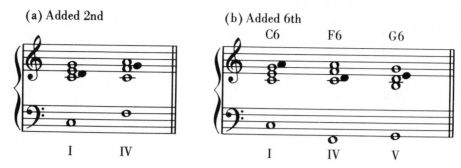

I   IV

C6   F6   G6

I   IV   V

In Example 11–18*a*, a melody is harmonized with chords containing added tones. The black noteheads in the reduction beneath Example 11–18*b* indicate the added 2nds and 6ths. Such added-tone harmonies occur in various twentieth-century styles.

EXAMPLE 11–18

(a)

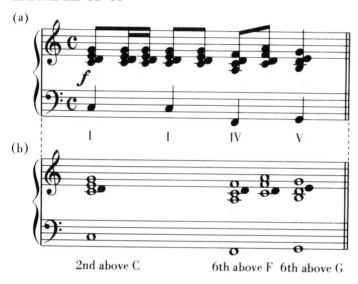

I   I   IV   V

(b)

2nd above C   6th above F 6th above G

Quartal Harmony

While tertian harmony involves chords built in 3rds, *quartal* harmony refers to chords based on 4ths. Quartal harmonies (Ex. 11-19*a*) produce a pleasant effect and are often included with other types of chords in compositions. Sometimes what appears to be quartal harmony is created by the spacing of the chord tones in tertian harmony. In Example 11–19*b*, the harmony is really a C9 chord (see Ex. 11-16*c*) with the 5th and the root doubled in the upper voices.

EXAMPLE 11–19

(a)

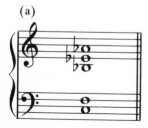

(b)

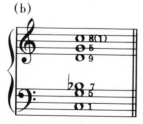

CHAPTER TWELVE
More Variation and Improvisation Techniques
Creating Accompaniments; Developing Motives

Accompaniments

Many of the harmonizations in previous chapters were in a keyboard style with three notes on the treble staff and one on the bass staff. In each case the melody tones were treated as the uppermost notes of chords. In such harmonizations, the notes on the upper staff are played by the right hand, while the notes on the lower staff are played by the left hand. In another effective keyboard style, only the melody is written on the upper staff, and the harmony is on the lower staff. In Example 12–1a, the opening melody of "Joy to the World" is harmonized with three notes on the upper staff and one on the lower staff. These chords are transferred to the left hand in the

EXAMPLE 12–1

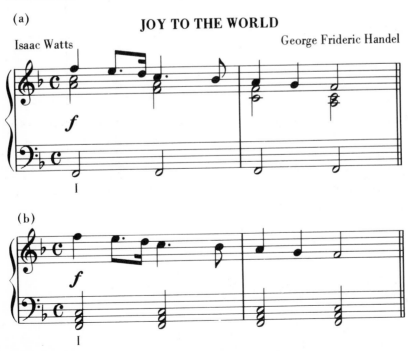

(a)

JOY TO THE WORLD

Isaac Watts   George Frideric Handel

(b)

keyboard format in Example 12–1*b*. Notice that the harmony in the left hand does not necessarily have the same arrangement of the chord tones as does that in the right hand.

Harmonies in the left hand may be sounded in a number of ways to create effective accompaniments for the melody in the right hand. For example, the basic triads in the left-hand accompaniment in Example 12–2*a* are given some rhythmic interest in Example 12–2*b*. In Example 12–2*c*, the tones of these harmonies are sounded separately, helping to reinforce the pattern of strong and weak beats. In this accompaniment, a single tone occurs on strong beats, while the remaining chord tones are played on weak beats. In Example 12–2*d*, the harmonies in the accompaniment are *arpeggiated*, or stated melodically. Since they supply rhythmic interest without distracting from the principal melody, these arpeggiations make excellent accompaniment figures.

EXAMPLE 12–2

Motives

Most compositions do not consist merely of continuous strings of new ideas but are organized around the repetition, expansion, and variation of units called *motives*. Defined as the smallest recognizable rhythmic and/or melodic pattern in a melody, a motive acts as a tiny building block that composers may restate, alter, fragment, and expand. The brackets in Example 12–3*a* and *b* indicate the motives in each of the phrases.

EXAMPLE 12–3

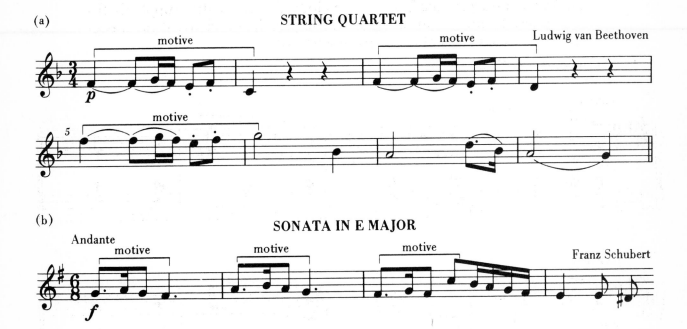

(a)   **STRING QUARTET**

Ludwig van Beethoven

(b)   **SONATA IN E MAJOR**

Franz Schubert

Melodic Development

The manipulation of motives is a basic means for building longer compositions. Often referred to as *melodic* or *motivic development*, this technique is especially notable in the works of well-known composers in the classical period (from around 1770 to 1830).

In the third movement* of his piano sonata Opus 10, No. 1, Beethoven states in the opening melody a motive that is easy to remember (Ex. 12-4). Later in the movement this motive is varied in several ways. In measures 5 and 6, for example, it is restated on a tonal level different from that of the beginning; then in measures 7 to 9, it is altered and expanded. In measures 47 to 53 (Ex. 12-5), the motive is stated, fragmented (abbreviated), and overlapped. Numerous statements of the fragmented motive in close succession greatly increase the intensity of the music at this point. While these altered motivic statements provide contrast and freshness, their unmistakable connection to earlier material unifies the movement.

---

*A *movement* is a distinct and relatively independent division of a larger work such as a symphony or a sonata.

EXAMPLE 12–4

SONATA IN C MINOR

Ludwig van Beethoven

FINALE
Prestissimo

EXAMPLE 12–5

The degree to which contrast and variety are balanced has traditionally been one criterion for judging the effectiveness of compositions in some styles. If totally new material is presented continually throughout a composition, the music may seem to wander, and the listener may become confused. Too much exact repetition, however, may be boring. While nearly all of the melodic material in the sonata movement described earlier may be traced to the opening motive, Beethoven's skill in motivic development renews the music and gives it vitality.

Although melodic motives are developed extensively in the hands of the great composers, such patterns are usually present in simple melodies as well. The melody of "O Come, Little Children" (Ex. 12-6) is based on a single motive, the rhythm of which occurs several times in all four phrases. The melody in phrase 2 is an exact repeat of phrase 1, and while phrases 3 and 4 have contrasting tonal material, the continuous statements of the rhythm pattern of the motive assure unity throughout the entire song.

EXAMPLE 12–6

O COME, LITTLE CHILDREN

C. von Schmidt

J.A.P. Schulz

Phrase 1

O come, lit - tle chil - dren, from cot and from hall,

Phrase 2

O come to the man - ger in Beth - le - hem's stall,

Phrase 3

There meek - ly He li - eth, the heav - en - ly Child,

Phrase 4

So poor and so hum - ble, so sweet and so mild.

More Variation Techniques

In addition to the unifying rhythm pattern of the motive in "O Come, Little Children," its underlying tonal contours are significant as well (Ex. 12-7). The reduction of phrase 1 on staff *b* shows the chord tones in each measure. The tones on strong beats only—G, G, F, E—are shown on staff *c*. This scalewise pattern from the 5th degree down to the 3rd, then, is the underlying contour of the phrase. A fundamental variation technique involves maintaining the underlying melodic contour and harmonic progression while changing the embellishments and rhythm. Disregarding the text and using the contour on staff *b* as a starting point, you can construct a series of variations on this phrase. As long as you maintain

EXAMPLE 12–7

(a)

(b)

(c)

the downward scalewise contour on staff *b*, you can make changes in embellishments and rhythm without losing the essential nature of the melody. Although the variations in Example 12–8*d* are by no means exhaustive, they demonstrate a few of the possibilities.

EXAMPLE 12–8

a. The melody is harmonized in keyboard style.

O COME, LITTLE CHILDREN

C. von Schmidt

J.A.P. Schulz

b. The harmony is transferred to the left hand.

c. Several accompaniments are created:
   (1) The rhythm of the accompaniment consists of steady eighth notes. The first beat of each measure is emphasized by a single tone.

   (2) The (♩ ♫) rhythm pattern in the melody is balanced with a ♫♩ pattern in the accompaniment. The result is an overall steady movement of eighth notes.

(3) The chords in the accompaniment are arpeggiated in an even eighth-note pattern, except for measure 3. In that measure, the longer duration of the tone on the second beat slows the momentum before the pause at the end of the phrase in measure 4.

d. Several melodic variations, each with a different accompaniment, are presented:

(1) Passing tones embellish the melody.

(2) Additional passing tones and a new rhythm pattern (♪ ♫) produce a new motive. A simple chordal accompaniment provides an appropriate support.

(3) The ♪. ♪ rhythm creates a distinctive motive for this variation.

(4) An additional motive (♪ ♪ ♪ ♪) gives variety to the melody. Notice that this motive is reflected in the accompaniment.

❮EXERCISE 12-1   Using Example 12–8 as a guide, make several variations on the following melodies as requested.

1.

TOM DOOLEY

American Folk Song

Hang down your head, Tom   Doo - ley.   Hang down your head   and   cry.

Hang down your head, Tom   Doo - ley   Poor boy, you're bound to   die.

a. Continue the harmonization of "Tom Dooley" in keyboard style. Write the chord symbols beneath.

b. Continue the harmonization by placing the chords in the left hand. Write the chord symbols beneath.

c. Make a variation of the accompaniment in the left hand. Refer to Example 12–8 for suggested patterns.

d. Make a melodic variation of "Tom Dooley." Use an appropriate accompaniment in the left hand and place chord symbols beneath.

e. Make an additional melodic variation of "Tom Dooley." Choose an accompaniment style different from the one used in *d*. Write chord symbols beneath.

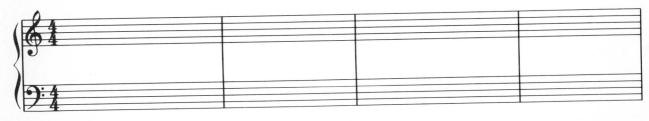

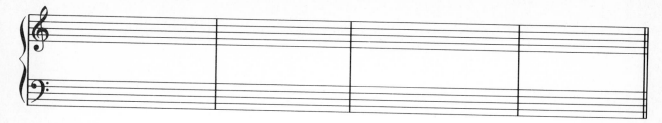

2.

WHEN THE SAINTS GO MARCHIN' IN

Spiritual

Oh when the saints _____ go march-in' in, _____ Oh when the

saints go march - in' in, _____ Oh Lord, I

want to be in that num - ber _____ When the

saints go march - in' in. _____

a. Continue the harmonization of "When the Saints Go Marchin' In" in keyboard style. Write the chord symbols beneath.

b. Continue the harmonization by placing the chords in the left hand. Write the chord symbols beneath.

c. Make a variation of the accompaniment in the left hand. Refer to Example 12–8 for suggested patterns.

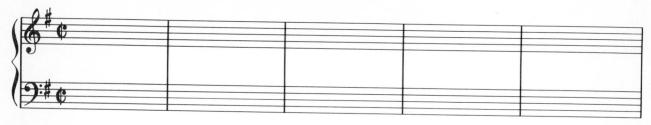

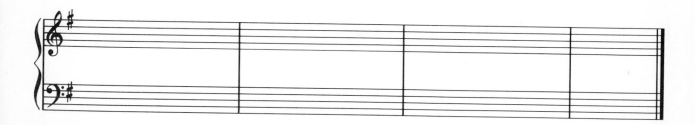

d. Make a melodic variation of "When the Saints Go Marchin' In." Use an appropriate accompaniment in the left hand and place chord symbols beneath.

e. Make an additional melodic variation of "When the Saints Go Marchin' In." Choose an accompaniment style different from the one used in *d*. Write chord symbols beneath.

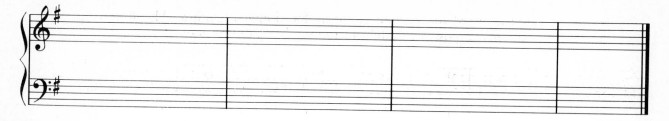

Options for Further Study

Improvisation

If you play an instrument or sing, you may wish to *improvise,* or perform extemporaneously, your own variations on some simple melodies. When you improvise on a given melody, you will apply the same skills learned earlier in writing variations. You should maintain underlying tonal contours and harmonic progressions while changing embellishments and rhythms.

◀EXERCISE 12-2   Create your own improvisations on the melodies in Exercise 12-1. Remember that accompaniments may be improvised as well.

Composition

To carry the creative process even further, try to compose your own melody. An eight-measure period is probably a good length for your first attempt. Below are some suggestions to follow:

1. You may devise your own rhythm patterns or set a text. (If necessary, refer to the section on rhythm in Chapter 1.) The following sample is not based on a text:

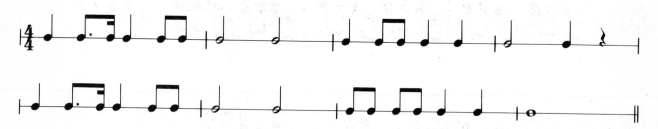

2. After deciding upon a key for your melody, experiment with underlying tonal contours similar to those in the songs in this chapter. Remember that both scalewise motion and outlines of the tonic triad (1st, 3rd, and 5th

scale degrees) make good contours for simple melodies. The following contour is a possible match for the rhythm patterns above:

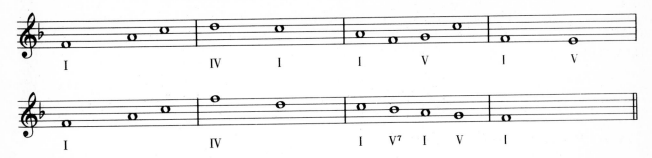

3. Compose your new melody. Chord tones are often placed on strong beats—for example, on beats 1 and 3 in $\frac{4}{4}$ meter. The rhythm of the melody will help to determine the number and type of embellishments. In the sample, compare the contour and the rhythm of the antecedent phrase with those of the consequent phrase:

4. Add an appropriate accompaniment for your melody; refer to Example 12–8 as needed. Below is a sample accompaniment:

❰EXERCISE 12-3   On the staves provided below, write your own melody and add an accompaniment.

Index